Running Without the Devil

Dedication:

To all those who have dared to confront your demons. It is time to savor your world. Enjoy every moment of your new life.

Acknowledgments

I have to take a moment and pause to thank everyone that stood by me during the worst hours of my journey. To my counselors, my wonderful wife, my son, my bosses and co-workers—and everyone in the running community that supported me in my recovery.

I would especially like to thank my wife Alejandra, and my mother Janice for never giving up on me. If it were not for my wife, I would be half the man I am today. I would not have had a wonderful child, I would not have found running, I would probably be dying a slow and painful death, or worse. She saved me, she shaped me, she is the rock, she keeps me grounded, she guides me.

D1606589

Thank you Mom for all the love over the years, always bailing me out, and always being there for me despite all my faults, behavior, wrong doings. Thank you for your unconditional love. I want to thank Sebastian for teaching me how to be a Dad, I love you buddy!

Quotations from *Alcoholics Anonymous World Services, Inc,4th Edition* ©2001.
Front & Back cover Photo: Progress Through Photography (ptpusa.org)

Foreword

Henry Ward isn't a therapist. He isn't a psychiatrist. He's not an expert in psychology.
This isn't a book about what he learned in books or in school.

Henry is an addict. He is a runner. He is an inspiration.
This is a book about what he learned in real life in the real world.

He battled addiction. He fought his demons.
He hasn't won, but he's winning. And this is his story.

He looked inward to understand himself, his motivations, his personality, and his unique strengths. He reached outward to build meaningful relationships, encourage new runners, help other addicts, raise money for nonprofits, and increase awareness about mental health challenges.

He climbed upward both literally and figuratively. He climbed out of the darkness and despair of addiction. He also climbs the mountains around Phoenix almost daily. He's rarely alone while he does this. He's a magnet for beginning and experienced runners, for those struggling with addiction and for those who aren't.

Addiction will drag you downward. The pain and fear will pull you backward.
Let Henry's journey push you forward. Always forward.

David Rendall
Professional speaker, Ultra Marathon Runner, 6 time Ironman Finisher and author of 5 books including the Freak Factor.

Table of Contents

Chapter 1: Growing up: The Die was Cast

Chapter 2: Living in Hell Part 1- 1987 The birth of My Drinking Career:

Chapter 3: Pick Your Poison: Booze or Weed

Chapter 4: European Health Spa/Let's Get Sober

Chapter 5: Running with the Devil

Chapter 6: Endurance- Street Hockey/Basketball, Not Wanting to Sit

Chapter 7: Expanding my Horizons: Beers, Weed and 'Shrooms

Chapter 8: 99 Trip Around the US in an RV

Chapter 9: Three DUIs in Hit-And-Run Acidents

Chapter 10: Culinary School:Another Shot at Getting Sober

Chapter 11: Move to Arizona; Running Away

Chapter 12: Marriage, Commitment Pact, Living in Hell Revisited

Chapter 13: 2008 Beijing Olympic Games Project

Chapter 14: Rock Bottom, November 17, 2008: Time to Face my Demons Head On

Chapter 15: November 19, 2008 - Valley Hope, Tempe, Arizona

Chapter 16: Now Back to My Marital Situation

Chapter 17: Therapy

Chapter 18: March 2009

Chapter 19: Move Back to Boston

Chapter 20: Alejandra's Move to Boston November 2009

Chapter 21: Squirrelly: Running with a Squirrelly Devil

Chapter 22: Life Quickly Changed- Seven Dwarfs Motel. July 2011

Chapter 23: Arizona February 2013; New Time zone; More Distance Walking

Chapter 24: Instead of Climbing the Walls, I Spent Time on Google Maps

Chapter 25: 2012 Boston Marathon

Chapter 26: 2013 Boston Marathon

Chapter 27: The Real Birth of my Running Career- Early May 2013

Chapter 28: RAW SERIES 6-1-2013

Chapter 29: Changing one Addiction for Another- 5k Races

Chapter 30: Forced Change Again-Laid off July 2013

Chapter 31: Obsessive, Compulsive, Addictive New Habit

Chapter 32: Can I Make my Running Hobby a
Career? Corning, NY October 2013

Chapter 33: The Cannoli Run- Enjoying my Long
Adventures!

Chapter 34: Full Marathon- December 2013

Chapter 35: Transition to Ultra-Run to Work from
Home

Chapter 36: Runwell- October 2016

Chapter 37: 12 Hour Treadmillathon - 2-18-17
Corning, NY

Chapter 38: Next Stop, my First Ultramarathon:
Manchester to Monadnock 5-1-16

Chapter 39:What Else Can I do with Runwell?

Chapter 40: Running Without The Devil/ Portland
Marathon 10-2-16 Birthday 15th Marathon BQ
(Boston Qualified)

Chapter 41:Javelina Jundred- My 1st 100 mile race
October 29, 2016

Chapter 42: National Personal Training Institute ,
Waltham, Massachusetts October 3, 2016

Chapter 43:12 hour Treadmillathon Corning, NY 2-
19-17

Chapter 44: Boston Marathon Quad April 1st,2017

Chapter 45: 24 Hour Track Run, Belmont, MA 4-25-17

Chapter 46: Moving to Arizona; Breaking My foot June 2017

Chapter 47: The Road to Patagonia;Almost There!

Chapter 48: Boston Marathon Quad 4-15-18

Chapter 49: Mesa Marathon Quad 2-8-19

Chapter 50:Running Without The Devil

Chapter 51: How Running Has Helped Me

Chapter 52:No Finish Line

9

Introduction:

Hello, my name is Henry Ward and I am a recovering alcoholic, an addict and an ultrarunner who grew up in Waltham, Massachusetts, and currently resides in Chandler, Arizona, with my wife Alejandra, my son Sebastian, and our dog Wini. I have been in recovery since November 17, 2008. I have been married to my beautiful wife for 16 years, and we have an adorable nine year-old son. I am a chef by trade and I love to run. Sounds normal enough, right? But this so-called normal life wasn't always the case. I am an ordinary human with an extraordinary story. I want to give back, I want to help others gain strength to seek treatment and recover from alcohol and drug addiction. I believe this is my mission. The purpose of this book is to show you that addicts can change and addicts can recover and often thrive in society.

For 22 years, I abused drugs and alcohol. I should be dead. I had numerous drug and alcohol-related arrests. I almost lost my family. I almost lost my life. Alejandra really had no idea who she was in a relationship with early on, but she is a very intelligent woman. We got married in June 2005, and later that summer our problems started to really escalate. The problems all were stemming from my drinking. We had so many discussions and arguments about why I had to drink, or why I drank so much the night before-- and where I was getting the money from to drink so much. It was tense all the time. She had made it clear that she did not like the person I was when I was drinking.

"I was pushing her away one beer at a time, one day at a time."

10

I remember picking her up from the ride-share from work most days, with several beers in my system. Even though I showered, brushed my teeth a few times and chewed gum she always knew I was drinking. I could not stay sober from the time I got out of work until I had to pick her up, which was really puzzling for her. It was always an uncomfortable discussion on the way home. When we got home, it was time to crack another one which prompted more questions and stress. Then of course when we went out to eat, I had to have at least 2, and when we arrived home, I would have as many as I could sneak or get away with. This daily routine put a tremendous strain on our marriage. I was pushing her away, one beer at a time, one day at a time. I knew she loved me; she just did not love Henry the drinker. I put her through hell, and she to this day has never given up on me. She continued to work on and to protect herself.

Our finances were a mess, as budgeting and financials were not my strength. It certainly did not help if I was constantly robbing Peter to pay Paul. I was constantly trying to figure out new ways to get money to buy alcohol without her knowing. I remember that I used to buy things at Home Depot and return them, and they would give you cash. I started doing this scam and started buying less expensive items, and then got greedy and started buying more expensive items and returning them for cash. Eventually Home Depot caught on, and so did Alejandra. There was no extra money in our tight budget for years, so the addict in me had to keep finding ways to get money. Getting cash back at the supermarket was another way. I would buy something for $2.00 and get $20 back and buy beer. Eventually this caught up to me as well, and losing $50 here and there from Home Depot, and $20 cash

11

back from the supermarket a few times a week really contributed to our debt.

I pride myself on not telling lies, but while in active addiction I was dishonest and would stretch the truth. "I only had a few beers" was the truth--though they were liters, and I also had tequila and rum...

I used to pray to God for all the wrong reasons. I remember watching a woman hop out of her car early one morning at my work and saw her drop some money as she rushed into the building. I was behind her, and when I noticed, I reached down and in one clean swoop I grabbed the money and shoved it in my pocket. I got in the elevator and counted it, $260! Shortly after returning to my kitchen at work the same woman frantically asked me if I found any money. I replied, nope, sorry but I hope you find it. That was my impulsive reaction. She said that I was the only one that could have seen it, to which I replied, "Sorry, cannot help you, I hope you find it though." I had prayed for money, and my prayers were answered! What a sick way of thinking. In my mind, it was found money, and I could buy the 2 new CD's I wanted, a bag of weed and have beer money for at least a week! The money was dirty, and I actually felt guilty every time I used it. I felt like such a horrible person for not giving the money back.

The biggest challenge of my life came when I finally admitted my addiction and sought help. I made one of the best decisions in my life by checking myself into Valley Hope of Tempe addiction treatment center. That was November 2008, and I have been sober ever since.

"If I could quit drinking or smoking, I believe I can now do anything."

You may be thinking, "I've heard this story before—or one that sounds like it. Why is my story different from others? I believe that I was given a special gift from God, and that gift is a superpower. When I am going through a tough stretch in a grueling running event or in life and I feel like I cannot go on any further, I can dig deep and think back to the hard times I had while I was drinking and using, and know that if I got through those times, I can get through a really rough patch in a race, or a tough day or stretch of days. It was much harder back then. If I could quit drinking or smoking, I believe I can now do anything.

Running has been critical in my recovery. After becoming sober in 2008, I found running in 2013. Although I knew deep down inside that I wouldn't use or drink again, I still had a void in my life that needed to be filled. During the two years leading up to May of 2013, I was becoming a squirrely mess. I had no hobbies and a lot of built-up energy inside that needed to be released. Though I wasn't drinking or using, I became restless and sort of a dry drunk. I needed to do something. Once I found running, it became my new addiction.

It started when I asked my friend Enrique who we would be visiting if he would run an 8K race (Wineglass 8K) in Corning, New York, where he lived. He said he would run it if I did. "Sign me up," I told him! I didn't even know how far an 8K was at the time! Leading up to the big day, I had run twice while pushing my son Sebastian in his stroller, and we ran together for the race as well.

13

I quickly realized how enjoyable it was pushing myself to go further and knew early on I could be a distance runner. I registered for the Boston Athletic Association Half Marathon in October 2013. This was a big deal, and I could not stop thinking about it! I did well and knew after completing it, I wanted more. What is the progression and logical next step? A full marathon! I registered for the Pittsburgh Marathon, which took place in May 2014, and I really enjoyed the long-distance training runs leading up to the race. I then ran the Wineglass Marathon in October, and the following year, I ran *eight marathons*! I was hooked on this distance until I heard about ultrarunning. My first question was, "Why would anyone want to run more than 26.2 miles?" I started asking questions, joining groups and reading about this ultrarunning thing. My first ultra was Manchester to Monadnock in May, 2015. I thought I was prepared, but the reality was I had no idea what was to come. I enjoyed exploring the unknown areas of the ultra event, pushing myself past my perceived limits, and I learned a lot from it about myself, and about running. I was now obsessed.

"I used running to share my story of hope."

Once I started to have some success in my running, I realized it could give me a platform to share my story of hope. I signed up to do a stage race in Patagonia, Argentina, in 2017 and started raising funds for Runwell, an organization that encourages running and fitness as part of the recovery process. I wanted to do some out-of-the-box fundraising concepts as a way to reach large audiences. The media got a hold of the story and did some news segments and articles. Within a span of six months in 2017 I did a three hour spinathon at my gym, 12 hour treadmillathon in my friend's gym in Corning, New York, the Boston Marathon quad (which is the marathon course four consecutive times), a 24-hour track run, and a 24-hour desert run, raising $12,000 for Runwell, with the money going directly to people who need treatment for addiction and cannot afford it. I have continued using my running platform to raise funds and awareness to fight addiction and have now done two 24-hour desert runs in the middle of the hot Arizona summer, four Boston Marathon quads, and three Mesa Marathon quads as fundraising efforts and most recently, the Satan Sidewalk 66 hour treadmill event in which I ran for 66.6 hours and accumulated 204 miles.

As an addict, there is no cure. For addicts, there is no such thing as moderation. It is more, more and more! I have to be careful about being too obsessive and continuing to want more. I think it is important to be driven and to pursue new goals, but that can come at a cost. The most important thing for me is taking care of myself. The first thing I learned in recovery is to take care of myself first. If I do not take care of myself, I cannot take care of anyone else. I cannot take care of a job nor a home. Running is self-care for me, but in the same breath, if I run too much, I will distance myself from my family and our time together. Family is the second most important thing to me. I would be nothing without them. They are my world. Physically, if I run and race too much, I will break down. I know that. I need to cross train and build myself to last. I want to be running when I am 80! I need to have crazy goals; I just cannot have too many of them be running goals. As they say in recovery, "One is too many, and 1,000 is not enough." I need to pick my

15

battles and choose my events wisely. I am well aware that I am a work in progress, and sometimes need to be reminded by my wife to cut back the miles, or to have a rest day or days. I'll take this running addiction over the active addiction years all of the time.

"Running helps me live life on life's terms."

When I discovered running in May of 2013, my life drastically changed for the better. Running helps me live life on life's terms. When I start the day with a run, the whole day seems to flow better. An afternoon run can help burn off the craziness of a busy workday. I am living proof that second chances matter. I am on a mission to pay it forward. I try to tell people it's okay to be an alcoholic and an addict—as long as you are seeking to recover. Most alcoholics and addicts don't want to be the way they are. But there is help, and there is hope. If there's a tomorrow, there is hope. I want to help others to receive treatment. I want to expose them to a whole new world of clarity and optimism. I'm passionate about fighting addiction and serving those living in recovery. I honestly believe that you can do anything you want to do. Sometimes you just need help, treatment, guidance, and therapy. The first step is wanting to change. The second is to commit 100% to this change.

Chapter 1
Growing up: The Die was Cast

I grew up in Waltham, Massachusetts. I went to Waltham public schools and enjoyed playing sports and staying active with my friends. I had a hard time sitting still. It would take me less than 30 seconds to finish dinner. I knew once I finished dinner and as long as my homework was done, I could go out and play. Homework was never a priority, and I invested even less time on it than dinner. I would do it half ass, usually during another class to get it out of the way. I was more interested in running around and playing sports than school. School was boring to me and I did not enjoy most of it. As a result, I achieved mediocre results at best. I drifted. I had no real identity, no career aspirations. I was totally complacent. My mother did nag me, but I continued to just do the minimum I needed to do to get by in school. When it came to sports, I enjoyed them; I had lots of energy and I felt alive inside. I really didn't have any pressure for college until my senior year in high school.

Paper Route

As a young teenager, I had jobs. My first job was a paperboy. I had around thirty-five papers to deliver Monday through Friday in the afternoons. I lived on a hill, and just like homework, I would try and get it out of the way as fast as possible. I could run the entire route, figure out the fastest and most efficient route, and always tried to beat my fastest time of 32 minutes. When I finished that meant I could play. I can honestly say that this was the foundation of my endurance. Perhaps I was pushing and competing against myself back then which may have set me up for success in my running 40 years later. I would not get tired, and the hills became routine.

Not Wanting to go to School

Why would anyone want to do something that they don't like? This thought constantly went through my head, and still does to this day. I hated school. Correction, I enjoyed art class, and gym. The rest for the most part I had no use for. I felt I was forced to learn something that I would never need in life. If I did not need something, why learn it and why try? I am 200% or 0%. Nobody ever communicated learning as a form of skill building. I was always told that school was just about getting into college so I could get a good job.

Baseball, Sports cards, Candy, Pizza, OCD, Early Years of Addiction

Along with the paper route, I took on other jobs such as babysitting, raking leaves, and snow shoveling, to name a few. With most jobs, there were rewards such as money. I always felt great once I got paid. I had money more money than most of my friends. I would spend my money on baseball cards, candy and pizza. I had to have the most cards and became obsessed and addicted to collecting all sorts of sports cards. There were cards that I needed to have. I ate a lot of candy. I would go to the store multiple times per day, to buy more cards, more candy. It's like I could not help myself, because I really couldn't. The old saying that the money was burning a hole in my pocket applied to me. I started to see a problem at a young age. It was never enough; I always wanted more and was never satisfied. More, more, more... I would treat my friends to pizza. I would eat as many slices as possible. One time I remember eating a large pizza all by myself. I was never satisfied with two slices. If I opened a large bag of Doritos, I would have to finish the whole thing. Girl scout cookies, same thing. I should have noticed a pattern here....

People even told me back in the day, that alcoholism was hereditary, but I still had the "it won't happen to me" mentality. Truly, I firmly believe that my addictive personality came from my family, both genetically and environmentally. Still, it was my own fault for not controlling it.

Home living: I grew up in a middle-class family and surrounded by alcoholism. I hated seeing other people drink. I hated seeing other people drunk because I recognized that it made people obnoxious and incoherent. It was really hard for me to watch; I hated it. It made me very angry to see people like that. I vowed never to drink and never wanted to be like the people I witnessed not making sense, yelling, being obnoxious or just not present. Little did I know, this same description would soon be describing me.

Chapter 2

Living in Hell Part 1- 1987 The Birth of My Drinking Career

Before I began drinking, I was shy and lacked confidence. Once I started to drink, the alcohol depressed my inhibitions, so I came out of my shell. I recall the first real time we drank, well somewhat. We had someone of legal age purchase us a case of wine coolers, as I despised the smell and taste of beer. The first one was magical, as I enjoyed the warm glow and buzz I had felt. Each one felt better and better, unlike Doritos which made you feel lousier, and lousier, and lousier. I remember doing all sorts of whacked out things, such as thinking it was a good idea to slide down a looooong railing, only to fall all the way down over the jagged boulders below. I woke up outside in the rain on the porch with my back completely cut up and hurting, throwing up, with a huge headache. I actually thought, this is what you are supposed to do when you drink. I felt like a rock star, not a bum. Drink as many as possible, do stupid things until you pass out, deal with the hangover and do the same thing the next time, or even the next day. I did feel guilt, and felt embarrassed that I would black out, and not remember much. What fun is that, not remembering something?

"Alcohol gave me the feeling I could do anything."

Things like this were normal occurrences when I drank in excess. This was learned behavior. Somewhat. We are responsible for our own actions, decisions and our behavior, though I was starting to feel like "I could not help it." Most of the people I witnessed growing up drank in excess. I was already out of control. After the thunder stopped in my head, and I was no longer a human volcano, I started plotting the next hammerfest. Make no mistake. It wasn't

21

that I was getting away with something illegal or forbidden. It was just the feeling the alcohol gave me that I could do anything—what some folks call "beer muscles."

As the partying became more frequent, everything else in my life started to take a backseat. School, playing sports, and family were all neglected. I felt like a rockstar when I drank. I had found something that made me happy, and I enjoyed how it made me feel, I could "escape" and I felt like I could be myself. I was not myself; I was out of my mind. But in my mind, I was cool. I fell in love with alcohol. It gave me confidence that I was lacking before though. Little did I know at the time, but I was developing a serious dependency issue. If we could not find anyone to buy alcohol for us, I would be seriously bummed out. I recall stealing and drinking warm Knickerbockers (cat piss is better tasting) from my Dad's stash in the basement just to satisfy my developing habit.

Family Ties

I lived with my parents for the first 34 years of my life and there were constant arguments about what I was doing in my room, and how I got home or where I was. Most nights, or days I staggered in the door and tried to avoid contact with them or anyone at my house. I did not want the confrontation, but when confronted my reply was that I was not bothering anyone else. My mom especially did not like the person who I was becoming or who I was but never kicked me out. My relationship with them and my brother and sisters was almost nonexistent for years. I would avoid them quite often because I did not want them to see me in the condition I was in, or I did not want to hear what they had to say, like , "You have a serious problem." Family gatherings were occasions to drink, but I would always overdo it. I was always warned, not to

22

drink too much, or to stop, you have had enough. When they would get on my case, it would piss me off and make me want to drink more. Nobody tells me what to do. And eventually if I did not stop drinking, I would be asked to leave.

Guidance Department

This high school department was a complete joke. Students were required to see their guidance counselors a few times per year or as needed, especially senior year. Guidance counselors were there to "guide" students to a career path. I honestly felt that unless you were an honor student, a jock, or someone special, they did not give a rat's ass about you. I slipped through the cracks for sure. Mr Jacobs was my guidance counselor. The guidance department's main job is to guide students, especially seniors in choosing a career for college or a trade school. I had really no skills, or desire to go to college but society suggests this is what I must do. Mr. Jacobs asked me what I wanted to do as a career, and I mentioned initially I wanted to be a baseball player, then sell baseball and sports cards, and then I did not know. I asked him what my hobbies were, and I told him about playing with my friends and hanging out! I am not sure what he thought of this, but this is when he determined I was destined for a career in liberal arts! I was a lost soul at him helping me. The only reason a young age and wish I had someone who guided me into an actual career or trade. Nothing against Mr. Jacobs, he had a couple hundred other students to help as well, I was just a number, and I certainly did not insist on him helping me. The only reason I went to the guidance department was because it was required!

I remember my counselor (just like my parents and society) told me that I needed to go to college and should try "Liberal Arts." What the fuck is liberal arts? Liberal Arts. I did not feel like I was being guided by them at all. My parents were pushing me to go to college as well. They had less suggestions for my "career." No offense to my parents, I had zero ideas either to contribute. Here we go again, being forced to learn or do something that I did not want to. Besides, if I went to college, wouldn't my new hobby of partying suffer?

Chapter 3
Pick Your Poison: Booze or Weed

Until 1988, which was my senior year of high school, I was totally against smoking weed and drugs in general. I saw what it had done to some people I knew and wanted no part of it or them. At the time, I saw how drugs changed people, but not alcohol. Maybe I was in denial. Then, for some reason, one day this changed. Perhaps it was curiosity, but I decided that I was ready and wanted to try smoking weed. I loved it. No hangover, not too many side effects, I thought it was perfect. I was drinking less, smoking more at this point, though it was becoming an expensive habit for a soon to be college boy. It was working for me.

Aquariums and Pet Stores
"Everything I was interested in I was addicted to."

Once I stopped really eating candy and obsessively collecting sports cards, I changed from those addictions to collecting fish, visiting pet stores and aquariums, and maintaining several fish tanks at my parents' house. I think the most I had was 7 at the time. We would go to the pet store pretty much every day and couldn't just go and not come home with a fish. I was obsessed with having all the fish that I wanted, especially aggressive fish. We got stoned and literally would go to the pet stores most days to see if any new fish came in. We would always be smoking weed on the way there and the way back, and this is how we spent our days. I actually drove to the pet store stoned and by some miracle, didn't get caught. I spent all my money on weed, fish, fish food, feeder fish, fast food for myself. Whatever little money was left over would go in the gas tank. I was addicted to aquarium fish! We did this during the week and on the

25

weekends, we drank like fish. I felt like I was Beavis or Butthead in real life. It seemed like everything I had an interest in I was obsessed or addicted to, even aquarium fish.

Chapter 4
European Health Spa/Let's Get Sober

A friend and I decided to join a gym. I was probably 6´feet tall and 125 pounds soaking wet. I was skinny. I really wanted to gain like 200 pounds of muscle at the time, but deep down inside, I believe I needed change. I started not liking feeling like shit all the time and I really deep down wanted to change my behavior, never mind change my body composition. I needed to run away from the partying lifestyle. I needed to stop putting a hole in my stomach all the time, cease being arrested for DUI and possession of a controlled substance. I felt humiliated and briefly remorseful over the DUI arrest, but then had myself a pity party over the expensive experience. I needed a clear head. After all, how was I going to succeed in a friggin' liberal arts career? I still did not even know what the F liberal arts was, but what I did know was that the gym made me feel GREAT! I was tired of feeling that lack of confidence. I saw the benefits of taking better care of myself. Exercise looked like a way to cut down on the drinking. I was convinced that if I looked better, I would feel better.

I started gaining muscle and looking better but felt like a million bucks. I had stopped drinking for a few weeks for the most part. I started drinking protein drinks, eating healthier, and was on my way to a lifestyle change. Then, I thought it would be awesome if I smoked weed before going to the gym. It would put me in the zone, and I would eat more to recover, and have more gains! Well, that worked--kind of. I forgot to take into account that weed was expensive for a part time worker, who had to pay for his car, car

27

insurance, gym monthly payment, food, and gas. First, if I did not have weed, I would not go to the gym. Secondly, my gas tank was usually empty and I ran out of gas more than 10 times because my priorities were way out of whack. Third, I would intentionally not pay for the car insurance, in the hope that the bill got lost on their end, which ended in three cancelled policies. I was delusional and immature. Only later did I recognize my immaturity in retrospect. My thought process was way out of whack and my judgement was clouded to say the least. Weed and alcohol were stunting my growth as a young adult, mentally and spiritually.

While my problems were of my own making, the Boston area was an uptight, dark cold, negative place where people didn't smile much. That probably affected my overall mood. I managed to get by and kept going to the gym most days. I really enjoyed the way I felt while I was there, but mostly after. The endorphins were kicking, which gave me a better attitude, and outlook on the day, and life in general. I will say at that time I did not enjoy running or cardio at all. I think it may have something to do with being winded after thirty seconds on the elliptical or bike due to smoking. F this, what do I need to do this for? I don't and won't do anything that I don't like. My thought process was that I will lose weight, not gain so I mostly stuck to the weights.

Not able to sit through class in Framingham State College

By this point, I am regularly using both alcohol and pot. Both were now easier to access. I was bored as hell in college, wondering why on earth would anyone want to learn the shit they were pushing

28

down my throat. Population, food and technology? That was a class that I had to take because everything else was full. My last name begins with W, and I was a freshman, so proposed schedules were submitted from seniors down to freshmen, and alphabetically from there. I got the worst schedule, and worst classes. I had macro and microeconomics, and calculus to go along with population, food, and technology. All of the above, I hated. I had large gaps between classes as well. I was fortunate enough to meet some friends in my classes who had similar interests as me, such as not going to classes, and smoking pot, and drinking during the day! I had no clue why I couldn't keep my grades up. It might have had something to do with not going to class, not studying, and partying my ass off instead? I believe that is what happened. I was placed on scholastic probation. Same thing happened in the second semester. Shitty classes, shitty schedule, shitty attitude. At least I had made new friends and was having fun.

"I was a lost addict that needed to find my way, the hard way. "

The following school year, I decided that I would try going nights, instead of full time in the day. This was more or less useless, because I would get high the entire drive up to school, only to fall asleep during every class. I don't recall what classes I took, but I do know that I was simply going to college because that was "what I was supposed to do." I have always struggled with the concept that one NEEDS to go to college. Don't get me wrong, education is very important, but college is not for everyone, especially me. Go figure, I did poorly. I was a lost addict that needed to find my way, the hard way.

29

You might wonder why my parents would pay for college if I did so poorly. It was my mother that insisted I go to college. She gave me three chances to make it. But, as I think about it now, by paying for college she enabled my behavior. I never considered any alternatives to college either. I had no other career paths. Trades didn't interest me. A plumber? An electrician? Not for me, thanks. I did want to become a pro baseball player at one time but knew that would not happen. I thought about turning my hobby into a business and maybe opening a baseball card store, but there were so any that it became too competitive. Overall, this lifestyle I chose was just plain boring and unfulfilling.

My relationships with some friends changed once I was 21. I did not really hang around with anyone if they did not drink in excess, and /or smoke weed. I would not go to restaurants like Panera if the restaurant did not serve alcohol. If a group of friends said they were going to a place like Panera, I recall just going home because there I could get a bite to eat and drink like I wanted to. There was nothing there for me at Panera. Just eating would kill my buzz. I started pushing certain friends away. I would make excuses as to why I could not hang out with them, basically because they did not smoke weed or drink a lot, which is really the only things I wanted to do!

"If I had gotten help back then, I would have matured quicker"
Now as I think about it, if I could travel back in time, what would I tell my 21 year-old self? You have a problem; there's a pattern. You need help; you need treatment. Don't wait. Don't suffer in silence. If I had gotten help back then, I would have matured quicker and

30

been on a better career path. Instead, I isolated. I saw others graduating and starting careers, having success, getting married, starting families and buying homes. They weren't around to do the things we used to do so I entertained myself. I drank by myself and nobody would bother me about my drinking. I was both envious and embarrassed that they were moving on. I was frustrated over my lack of success. I felt stuck. I didn't know what to do. I had no direction. I didn't get help, even though I knew I couldn't stop on my own. I was ashamed and embarrassed. I didn't know anyone else who had gotten help.

Chapter 5

Running with the Devil

"We put ourselves in danger, just for a little weed."

By summer of 1990, I was running around with a different crowd, friends that always had weed and/or beer. Chris, Dan and myself had a blast ALL the time. Pretty much everything took a back seat to partying. I don't think there was a second of that summer when I was not high. We smoked joint after joint, bowl after bowl, bong hit after bong hit. It was a lot of fun living this lifestyle. I didn't have a care in the world. If there was nothing to do, we would just drive around aimlessly smoking the days away. Problem with this was we never had money, as all 3 of us were unemployed. Each day we would scrounge up enough money for gas, lunch, and a dime bag ($10 worth of pot) or more. We went to great lengths at times to find some. We HAD to start our days together by first of all obtaining pot. We would figure out the rest of the day later. We would drive to shady cities, ask homeless people, crack heads, complete strangers if they knew where we could score some weed. We put ourselves in danger numerous times, just for a little weed. We went to dangerous neighborhoods. I recall sitting in crack houses wondering what the fuck was wrong with us. We did this and basically we go to a pet store and just kind of hang out and look at and purchase aquarium fish. They probably did call us Beavis, Butthead and Todd... There was absolutely no plan for the future-- we lived for the day. Which ironically is what you are supposed to do especially in recovery!

"When I was not partying, I was miserable...the voices in my head were beating me up."

32

Little did I know at the time how much damage I was doing to my body, mind, and my image. I had a lot of fun, while I was partying, but when I was not, I was miserable. I started feeling remorse and guilt about blowing off things and events that should have been important to attend, or showing up tanked and embarrassing myself, and more importantly, my family. I would beat myself up pretty good afterwards, but then go right ahead and do the same thing over and over again. I felt like I couldn't help it. I would tell myself to have a drink or two to make myself feel better, and to stop beating myself up, but I could hardly ever stop at one or two. I drank to excess. I was becoming a mental case. I had to quiet the voices in my head, that were beating me up.

Mass Bay Community College

I decided to go back to college, so I registered at Mass Bay. My classes were better, and so was my schedule. This was another attempt to find myself and "sober up". However, my hobbies were still the same. School quickly became boring, and I hate to be bored. I had some friends from Waltham who went there and started hanging out with a few new friends with similar interests. Skipping school, smoking pot, and drinking. We also had a blast! I recall going to Boston University and basically breaking and entering into a building so that we could party for the day. Many other times we went into the old gym there and did the same thing. Not sure how we didn't get arrested, as we tore it up pretty hard, and literally tore up the place, breaking things in the process. My grades were poor, but my partying was great. Despite the damage I was doing, I was having a lot of fun. The problem later was that the last few years of drinking before I received treatment, it stopped

33

working for me. I was not having the fun I once was. I was really enjoying the college lifestyle, except that I wasn't smart enough academically to get by. One year and done with college forever.

Turning 21

Turning 21 was a monumental day for me. That meant that I had the freedom to buy alcohol whenever I freaking wanted to, which was scary, but pretty awesome at the time too. I did lose that adrenaline rush of trying to find somebody to buy for me, but I had everything readily available. Driving up to New Hampshire when their store is open at 6 AM on the weekends to purchase beer became fairly routine. I always felt ashamed doing this, but it became so routine, that is just what I did. So many Sunday mornings I would force myself to eat something and drink an iced coffee or two then I would make the drive up to New Hampshire to start my beer drinking for the day, earlier than later. I would ditch the iced coffee and crack a beer on the way down to Massachusetts and get ready to get nice and primed. Sometimes I would run out and have to go back which is obviously dangerous, but I was drinking more and building up a tolerance. It also meant that I didn't really need to find a party or find something to do, I could now entertain myself and I didn't have to go anywhere or get in any trouble--I could stay home and drink.

I could grab a 30-pack and go down to the park and drink there too. I love being outdoors, so I thought nothing of just hanging out in the park and getting hammered by myself. I started really isolating myself and did not want to deal with anything, which included people sometimes. This is when I really started noticing I was

34

developing a habit. I felt like a junkie or a bum. I really did not like who I was becoming, I felt like a scumbag sometimes because of my drinking. Just about every day was Thanksgiving or Groundhog Day, whatever you want to call it. Every day I was lit up. I do not and will not ever like being bored so I would entertain myself with beer and drugs and watch a little TV, listen to music, or both. Imagine if I had the internet back then? I would more than likely would have been an absolute terror on Facebook and other social media outlets embarrassing myself and others. I assume I would get sucked in every single post and negatively comment and fall deep into an abyss of social media negativity. I still went to parties, whenever I could. Before I went, I needed to make sure that there would be enough beer, or if I had enough beer first. That fear was always prevalent. I was becoming or was a professional drinker and addict. I spent too much time drinking and thinking about drinking, it became an obsession. My mind was cluttered.

Rollerblading to Boston, Billerica. What Lengths Would you go to Party?

I had lost my driver's license for the 2nd time and was pretty frustrated with life, myself, and pretty much the shitty situation I was in again. I felt stuck. People drink to be social and I did as well. Problem was and is, they can have one or two and I cannot, because I am an alcoholic and addict. What I didn't know then was that alcoholics are not only psychologically habituated to drinking, they become physically dependent on alcohol. It helped me gain such things as beer muscles, beer goggles, and beer confidence.

35

Beer gave me great motivation and encouraged me to come out of my shell and do things I normally would not do.

I had a few beers one Sunday morning and ran out. I felt possessed. I didn't know what to do so I got the bright idea of rollerblading to Billerica, Massachusetts. This was 14 miles away and was the closest place to buy beer on Sundays. I grabbed a backpack, my wallet, and one bottle of water and strapped on the rollerblades (without brakes) and recklessly made my way down the hill I lived on and headed north to Billerica. By the time I arrived I was pretty much proud of this accomplishment. I purchased a 24 pack of cans of beer, and it was time to reward myself. So, I found a park or something like that and proceeded to drink 3 or 4 beers and smoke some weed. I probably spent about 15 minutes there and then started my trek home. Problem now was I had a buzz, with a heavy backpack and it was really humid and then later there were periods of torrential downpours. Rollerblading and rain don't mix. Throw in some beer and you have a volatile situation. I fell down quite a few times and also my beers got all shaken up. The beers were basically undrinkable until I got back. I remember that I kept tapping the top of the can to keep the carbonation down, to no avail. I was wasting beer and got really frustrated. Pretty much all my beers were no good--all that way for nothing!

"I now had a bad problem I could not get rid of."
I had just gotten in over 30 miles basically only to drink a few beers and then have to wait about 24 hours for them to calm down before I could drink those said beers again. What was one to do? Well, I walked down the street after cleaning up a bit to drink heavily glass

after glass after glass after glass of dollar draft beers. Needless to say, that was a pretty impressive feat to think I had gone further than I had ever gone on Rollerblades. My legs were really not that tired nor was I winded even though I smoked. I always felt that I had this endurance gene. Yeah, I could hit the bike paths and easily do 25-30 miles, but it was a different challenge with all the elements and the heavy pack that I wasn't used to. Again, I asked you what lengths would you go to in order to get beer or drugs or anything? I could go to those lengths to get beer. What lengths could I go to actually quit drinking? I had to ask myself these questions later on down the road. I had a problem I could not get rid of. I now had it bad.

Being 21 and being able to buy beer I was drinking every day because it was convenient and because I could. But deep down inside it was because I had to. I developed a routine, more like a habit. I started feeling like I was possessed, like something inside of me was controlling me. I just had to buy beer and party. It had now taken over my life. It was who I was and I accepted it. I started to get scared sometimes that I could not stop. It was my identity and I was often ashamed and embarrassed of my image and at the time there wasn't a damn thing I could do about it. I honestly felt possessed and things were out of my control. Just like in recovery you have to accept that you have a problem and accept that you're powerless. I knew that I was powerless and did nothing about it at the time. I thought, maybe that's what I was supposed to be doing, I was supposed to be an alcoholic. I was supposed to party. That was me. I believe it was a lesson and this was true: without a struggle I wouldn't have found running and I wouldn't have found who I am today. Progress through a struggle helps you gain confidence, I had little progress back then.

Laps at the Park/I was Going Insane

I could do this over and over and over and over again. All day. Even though I was partying I was still able to keep going and going. In many ways I hid my drinking. I really don't enjoy being indoors. I like being outside but oftentimes I had nothing productive to do. All I felt like doing was drinking. I was going out of my mind being inside cooped up in a room behind closed doors. I had this anxiety that I needed to get out. I had a lot of potential energy that needed to get out. I was pretty good at rollerblading and would strap my rollerblades on and just do laps and laps down in the park from my house. It was almost a 1-mile loop. I would stash a backpack or a cooler with ice packs or ice and do a lap, chug a beer, do another lap, chug another beer and so on literally for hours. I was getting exercise in my mind and being productive but mainly I was moving so I wasn't going out of my mind like I was while "stuck" in a room. So, there were two positive things: I wasn't going batshit crazy inside and I was getting some exercise.

Imagine if I did this without drinking? What a crazy concept, what a phenomenon. But at the time I just couldn't. As mentioned before, I felt possessed--something was making me drink. The little voices in my head insisted on haunting me. I would not rollerblade nor would I ride my bike without being high or having a little buzz or a big buzz from a beer. Just wasn't as fun and my excuse was that I could not just let go and be fearless if I were not impaired. Beer gave me a false sense of strength that I was somewhat invincible so

38

I would go down the hill with no brakes, take corners and chances and risks I shouldn't have. I should be dead because of this alone. I scared the living crap out of myself and others with "near misses." I was careless and reckless. Though in retrospect it helped prepare me for some of the risks I need to take nowadays and not to be afraid. If I could do some of these things, make some of these choices while I was drinking then why couldn't I do it while I was sober? I could, but I just couldn't be sober. I can now because I am sober.

The Wave, $1 Drafts = Beer Marathon

I worked 3/10s of a mile from my home and the sports bar was right next door and my gym right below that. The sports bar called "The Wave" brought me such great joy. Money was one of my personal issues and they had dollar drafts. I got in a lot of trouble there. I went there because it was close, I enjoyed most of the regulars there and because of the amount of dollar drafts and the fact that I could duck out and smoke weed while I was there. Yes, they would over-serve you but that was on me as well. I would buy as many beers as I had time for, drink until I either passed out, threw up or was asked to leave. I was a paying customer and I was the one that demanded more. I can honestly say without bragging that I probably had over 20 beers every Sunday during football season and in between, 10 and 20 every other time I went there for the most part. If I ate anything while I was there it was something like mozzarella sticks or chicken fingers. It was fun for me to drink as many beers as possible and watch sports and hang out with my friends. I literally

39

participated in the "beer marathon" on several occasions. Not bragging but that's pretty good for a 145 lb 6' 2" male.

No regrets as I really had a good time when we went there, except that it really escalated my alcoholism. Problem was that while doing this of course I made poor decisions. I didn't have to drive home but most times I would because it was convenient. I had numerous fist fights and arguments in the bar and in the parking lot. I was asked to leave several times as well. I passed out on the steps, in my car, or at the bar. After something like that happened, I would be so ashamed, but would nervously come back soon and face the music and ridicule. I started building up a very bad reputation of being a clown and a drunk, a drug dealer, a bar fly which I thought was kind of cool, but obviously this was not very cool. I could certainly drink with the best of them, but I was also very sloppy, belligerent, loud, obnoxious, annoying and maybe not so fun to be around unless others were equally as wasted as I was. I became somewhat obsessed about going there because it was so convenient. The beers were so cheap and I knew people and people actually talked to me because some would be just like me. Perhaps we had something in common, most of us were alcoholics. We came here to get messed up, escape and drown our sorrows and problems in pint glasses or get away from our nagging loved ones. We navigated toward each other because we had a few things in common, sports and desire to get wasted.

I remember going to see Faith No More play at Avalon in Boston with a friend. Like all concerts, we would get really primed up first, and drink and smoke weed during the show and go slam dancing. The band was absolutely amazing from what I remembered, and I remember having a blast until halfway through the show. I remember all of a sudden feeling completely wasted and had the idea of climbing up on stage. I had a fanny pack on with money, 1 oz of weed, $$$ and my wallet and my friend's keys in it. I dove into the crowd and felt a tug on my shirt that was tied around my waste and when I fell to the floor, I realized someone had stolen my fanny pack with all those items in it!

"Alcoholics and addicts are never accountable for their actions."
My immediate reaction was shit, my beer money and all the weed! My friend's keys (which went to the car that we drove to the show) and my wallet were not my first thoughts. How was I going to drink the rest of the night and how was I going to get high? Oh, and then how was I going to get home following those questions. My friend was pissed and was not talking to me, even though "it was not my fault." Alcoholics and addicts are never accountable for their actions. I recall asking people who I did know to buy me beers after I told them my story of bad luck. I looked everywhere for my fanny bag and shirt, but no luck. I continued to drink and enjoy the show and wound up on the stage again, this time while missing one shoe. Basically, I had shorts on, and one shoe, no shirt and no money. At this point, security escorted me out. I explained to them my problem, and after the show that helped me look for my lost items, but no luck finding them.

Now what? It was time to find a way home (7 miles). No money, no shirt and one shoe. I started walking/running when I could, and eventually found my way to Waltham, and noticed the Sports Pub was open! I peeked in the window and saw two friends! They waved me in and I told them I had no shirt! One of them gave me his hoody, and I

41

went in and drank with them until the place closed, and they gave me a ride home. I had to work in the morning and was a complete mess. I stunk, I was still drunk, and I was still trying to piece together the night before. My friend whose keys I lost was saying that he had to have his car towed, pay for storage and get new factory keys made which in all totaled somewhere around $500 and was looking for me to pay for it. I was out my own personal money, $150 worth of weed, a shirt, basically a new pair of sneakers, my wallet, license and debit card. My concerns were: how was I going to drink when I got out of work if I had no money, or no debit card? How was I going to get more weed? This is an example of the madness that happened on a regular basis due to my out-of-control behavior while drinking. I made poor decisions and I was never accountable. Yes, someone stole my stuff, but I put myself in a position I should not have.

My relationships with some friends changed once I was 21. I did not really hang around with anyone if they did not drink in excess, and /or smoke weed. I would not go to restaurants like Panera if the restaurant did not serve alcohol. If a group of friends said they were going to a place like Panera, I recall just going home because there I could get a bite to eat and drink like I wanted to. There was nothing there for me at Panera. Just eating would kill my buzz. I started pushing certain friends away. I would make excuses as to why I could not hang out with them, basically because they did not smoke weed or drink a lot, which is really the only things I wanted to do!

I had some girlfriends and dated girls from the age of 18 to the age of 34 when I met Alejandra, but I was immature and not 100% vested in any of the relationships. I cared more about partying than my girlfriends. I often blew them off in lieu of a party. I spent more money on beer than them. I enjoyed being with them but enjoyed being messed up more. I dated barflies as well because they were doing the same things I was, just that deep down inside I was looking for a good girl to help me, and help me find myself and get sober, a barfly would never do that for me. There were a few years in my 20's that I would have to say that I was undatable. I was a mess. One of my best friends asked me if he could ask me a serious question. He asked if I was gay. I was like, what! He said, I never see you or hear you talk about girls. I told him that I was not gay, but just waiting for the right girl to come along. This was my excuse as this was my undatable period of time.

The same friend who only drank occasionally would also ask why I had to drink so much. This friend would try and help and offer advice, and I started pushing him away. We would go out for lunch together often and I always had a few beers 1st. I worked 3rd shift then and he worked 1st, so this was my nighttime." He could not comprehend as to why I had to drink everyday, and every time we went to lunch together. Short answer was that I am an alcoholic; long answer was because at the time I had to feel normal. I was pushing this friend away, I did not want him to give me any more crap about my drinking, so sometimes I would make up excuses as to why I could not go to lunch that day.

Never Rollerblading or Biking Sober

I have lost my license three different times with three different DUIs, all of which were hit and run. Part of the probation stipulations from these charges was to be abstinent from alcohol and drugs, and one of the times I was to enter a program and outpatient treatment center. All three accidents I was very intoxicated, and hit a car head on, another car head on, then a telephone pole head on. I am very lucky; as I spent time in jail overnight telling the cops I would never drink again. The next day I vowed never to drink again, and even the following day about never drinking again. I was sorry and remorseful, but I went to the store "just to get a six pack." I was feeling really sorry for myself and did what I knew to do best: drink to ease the pain, this is how I coped. I went on to drown my sorrows in several bottles of beer. Alcohol being a depressant, I felt more remorseful and guilty. After the second accident, I was ordered to attend an outpatient treatment center. I did not apply myself during my time there--I did not want to be there. In fact, every single Tuesday and Thursday I would meet my friend and we would drink some beers immediately after both of those sessions. I recall as I was nearing the end of the program I would drink even more because it was almost a celebration that it was over. It was time to graduate. Fake it until you make it. At least for two nights during the week while I was in the program I had less time to drink. And then of course it was back to drinking every night like I wanted to once I "graduated."

You would think 3 DUI's would be a wake-up call, right? Only briefly, at the time. Going to court, to jail, having no car—believe it or not, it was still not enough to get me to stay sober. I couldn't afford to lose my license for a year. The problem was, I just couldn't think straight.

44

When I left the scene, it was "fight or flight". I only cared about covering my ass. Yes, I ran away like a coward and thought I could get away with it. I only had remorse later. I eventually would start drinking and driving again because I had to drink, and I had to get from point A to point B. Initially I would "never do it again, I learned my lesson." But then I was back to doing what I was doing before, drinking and driving and jeopardizing my life and others. Was I numb? Did I not care? I think I just thought that I was an excellent driver that got careless, and that I would not get caught again. I was always a risk taker, what were the odds of being caught 3 times? I was not catatonic, or a sociopath, just delusional and not thinking clearly.

Chapter 6

Endurance- Street Hockey/Basketball, Not Wanting to Sit

I felt like I had built up some pretty decent endurance from rollerblading, I was biking all over creation and enjoyed playing pick up or organized sports on teams with friends. However, I never wanted to sit, or rest. When I rested, I stiffened up, but worse than that I became restless, and then mentally tired. If I could play the entire time that would be ideal, and most of the time I could. I found that I would lose my wind but regained it pretty quickly. Same thing for my legs, I recuperate quickly too. I was always a pretty good athlete but never really great in any particular sport, I was more of a dirt dog. I out hustled people and could play defense like you wouldn't believe. I would annoy the shit out of some of the top players, especially the ones that were taller than me. I played a very physical game, getting in your face and would back down from nobody. My goal was get in your head and intimidate you. I would hit you, pull your shirt, step on your foot. I was a pain in the ass and I probably still would be. The other players were pissed off. They noticed the smell of weed or beer on me but I didn't care. I thought they were just soft. I didn't think I was wrong.

Once I turned 21 and really liked to drink and smoke weed, I developed the bad habit of having to be intoxicated while playing sports. So the in your face mentality became intensified and perhaps over the top. I was not going to play unless I was high or had a few beers. It honestly elevated my game while it made me a lot more aggressive. Later, I reacted when they played aggressively. I certainly was sloppy at times but it didn't slow me

46

down. I used all the anxious energy inside me. I never wanted to sit and I always want to be part of the action. When you sit your buzz would wear off too, and that was no good... I would also lose my focus on my intensity which meant I either needed to keep playing or keep drinking and smoking weed.

By now I built up endurance from going to the gym and then rollerblading like a madman and riding my bike as well so playing a whole game of hockey or basketball. Even though I smoked I could get my wind back pretty quickly I'd recuperate pretty quickly. Just like at the bar scene, while playing pickup sports the way I was I'm sure I pissed off a lot of people and it wasn't just because I was an aggressive athlete. It was because I was fucked up. I would be belligerent and sloppy and people would get pissed off because at the end of the day people have to wake up and go to work in the morning. It was not fun for them to be continuously hit. It was fun for me but it probably wasn't fun for them. And at the time I felt invincible. I would get the benefits of the endorphins when I played sports just like the runners get a high from running. I really love to play.

Obviously, I can't take back time but I wonder what type of athlete I would have turned out to be if I didn't drink and didn't smoke weed while I was playing. What if I was just a sober athlete? I'll never know. What I do know is that I was pretty much a space cadet before I started drinking and smoking while playing sports. I was also pretty nervous being a smaller kid growing up (even thought I was six foot two by the time I was twenty-one). Same deal, beer and weed gave me the confidence to be myself to be as aggressive as

47

possible and let out aggression and run around like a fool as opposed to being timid, nervous and tentative like a smaller child and teenager. At a minimum, it gave me some courage.

Chapter 7

Expanding my Horizons: Beers, Weed and 'Shrooms

I started to hang around with people that got a little bit better quality weed. I discovered there were a lot greater potent types of weed and mushrooms out there than I was used to. Unfortunately, I couldn't afford potent weed and mushrooms and continue with my drinking career never mind afford food or anything else. So, I did what most intelligent people would do, which was get enough so that I could sell and offset the cost of mine. The more I sold the more I had for my head stash. I would not say I was ever a dealer, I just needed to pay for my habit. (Most dealers don't use drugs and most addicts don't deal. drugs.) To be sure, I wasn't a good businessman. I didn't keep track of what I sold and I didn't collect on my IOU's, so I lost money. The more of a head stash I had then what I consume or share, go figure. Even the most potent strains of weed you can build up a tolerance for and the same thing with the mushrooms. So, you needed to smoke more, get more, try different strands. This became a new obsession. I'd always pick up what's new and share. I would stock up and suddenly I became even more popular because I had what others wanted. Needless to say the more powerful the weed the more fucked up you get any more brain cells you kill the same thing with the mushrooms. So, there's a few years there I really walked around like a zombie because I was a zombie. Alcohol, weed, and mushrooms are all illicit drugs that kill brain cells. I always killed them at a rapid rate. I started noticing that my short-term memory was terrible which scared me. How bad was it? I didn't remember a concert I went to at all; I had a déjà vu; I couldn't even remember what I had for lunch or dinner. Will it

49

ever come back? I guess it didn't really matter because this is who I was and this is what I was going to do no matter what. I was going to party like a rockstar.

At the time I thought about writing a book about my fucked-up life not to help somebody but to kind of brag about how messed up I was but how much fun it was having to. Don't get me wrong I really did have a blast a lot of the time but there's also consequences for my actions and reactions to my actions. The arrogant me felt like I was progressing nicely in the partying world from beer to tequila to weed. It's a really good quality weed to mushrooms and then trying a few other things, but the other things really scared the shit out of me. I could see what it was doing to other people, I could see what it did to other people. I've heard all the stories and then once I tried a few other things I knew what they would do to me. Kill me or kill my soul. Deep down inside I knew it was bad enough that if I did that there might not be any turning back. This was the first time I had to let go of a few friends. Some of them were just people I would party with and weren't really friends in retrospect, but some of them were legitimate friends that I hung out with every day which was hard. But I didn't want to go down the path they went down and quite honestly I probably would have been dead. I was terrified of falling into that abyss. I would have liked it too much, that much I know. I've always had morals and a back bone and I couldn't see myself doing things like some others did such as robbing stores or houses, selling things just to get a fix, never mind how it changed some of their personalities. Getting into hardcore drugs completely took over some of my friends' lives rapidly. People I knew were starting to OD, people were dying, people went to jail for a long time. I was in pretty deep myself with just alcohol and mostly weed. Partying was a priority, one way or the other it is what I did. How much time do I have to drink, where am I drinking and what do I have to do the next day determines everything. Every day was Thanksgiving. I lived life like there was no tomorrow. I spent whatever money I had and didn't worry about the next day.

I have always been pretty angry and I was getting angrier and angrier and angrier and angrier and angrier as the days and months went on. I was spiteful and jealous of others who had more than me. I wanted what they had materially but in retrospect I wanted what they really had which was the ability to control themselves. I was out of control. I was driving myself nuts. I had some long spells of depression and anger with super negative thoughts. I had a pity party every day and I beat myself up pretty bad. The only way I really knew how to get out of my own head was to go out and rollerblade or go for a bike ride, but I would drink and smoke too. This became a daily thing--sometimes I would head out two three, four, times a day.

Music

I owe a lot to music for keeping me going. Just like everything else that I need an outlet. I have had some things come and go but music has been a constant for me, and a constant that almost works for me. It can help change my mood and can motivate me. I was always into music, mostly metal but anything really that made me feel good and move. I was addicted to CDs and concerts! I had to have all the CDs I wanted. Anything new that came out that I wanted, I got. Maybe obsessed might be a better description, but I

51

had to have new CDs, and had to go to most shows. After I stopped eating candy, collecting sports cards, my priorities shifted to new CDs, beer, weed, a little bit of extra money for gas and miscellaneous purchases. I had over 500 CDs. I went to every concert I wanted to go to. I have no regrets about buying all those CDs. I feel like there were many times that I was so bummed out music helped get me through those times. I love to listen to hardcore, punk rock, and metal. I enjoy music that I can feel, and music that I can relate to, music that I can get my aggression out to, music that moves me. Music that can change my mood. Music that can help me snap out of my funk. If I am going through a spell of depression and anger, I could relate to a lot of what they were saying in the lyrics and I could feel their music and it pushed me and kept me going. Music was a great outlet and still is today. It's less damaging than a lot of my other addictions and obsessions.

Back in the day, I loved going to live shows and hitting the mosh pit. To me this is a great way to get out my aggression, smashing other people harmlessly and showing off my beer muscles. The concerts were kind of like partying, sports, and music all in one little package. I would go to the shows with people that did the same thing I did which was partying our asses off beforehand, then continuing partying and running around with reckless abandon until it was time to drive home. Oftentimes I would drive home with reckless abandon which I am deeply sorry for risking anybody's lives, but these are some of the poor decisions that I continued to despite knowing the consequences. At the time, I couldn't help myself. At the time, I didn't feel sorry for engaging in risky behavior. I just kept doing it. If I had to get to a party or to get beer

52

or whatever I wanted to do, 99% of the time I was driving messed up. I looked at concerts almost like endurance events. The races were something to look forward to and were enough to keep me going. I always need something to look forward to, otherwise I tend to feel bored and complacent.

The summer was the best because most concerts were outdoors, and I love to be outdoors. Some of the large festivals such as the Ozzfest, The Warped Tour, and Lollapalooza were endurance events of their own. You wake up ready to party all day and night. There would be live bands for 12 hours and we would be partying under the sun party slam dancing all day. This would obviously require a lot of stamina and endurance. There were a lot of casualties and only the strong survive. Somehow, someway I always did. I do not know how I got home sometimes but I had the endurance to withstand the sun, standing all day and night, slam dancing all day! Almost every time I went to these places I drove and I'd always say I'm not going to drink when I go into the event knowing everything will wear off but what would happen was I would end up drinking while I was in there, and either be really really wasted all day or already starting to feel a hangover tired pass out and risk people's lives going home. It's obviously not a great plan but I did what I had to do because I was an addict and alcoholic.

Chapter 8
99 Trip Around the US in RV and the Aftermath

One of my close friends Jeff and his girlfriend Jen at the time were invited on a trip that involved renting an RV and camping and partying and spending the entire summer on the road and campgrounds all across the United States. I was asked to go and figured out a way to make it happen. I was really excited and this was another perfect opportunity to "change" my lifestyle. My goal was to relocate to California, or somewhere else. I needed a change. I needed a fresh start. I wanted to not feel like I was feeling and thought a geographical move would be the answer. Who am I kidding? Change? At that point I was not ready to change, not ready to be sober. How would moving or a trip keep me from drinking and using? I had more time on my hands, money, and freedom. Nobody was telling me what to do, no work, no real responsibilities to speak of. It was time to party more, and I was scared. I could not hide it anymore.

After attending Woodstock 99 in New York with my friend Jeff, we met up with the three ladies who drove the RV from Massachusetts to New York to pick us up. We were so glad to see them, and that is when the real party started. Every day I drank like a fish, often woke up and had a beer to kill the hangover feeling and start the day off right. This was quite alarming to Jen, and after a few days on the road she asked me if I drank every day, and I was like, "Not every day." "She said "Almost every day?' I said, "No, of course not." I clearly was lying to protect myself, but then there was no hiding it; I drank every damn day on that trip. When you live with or travel with people you really get to see who they are.

There might have been a day or two that I did not drink, but that was it. I was buzzed the whole time. She asked if I thought I had a problem and said that I just like to party, and I was on vacation. There were times on that trip that I was scared that I could not stop. Some of those days when I woke up and had a beer it was like I was doing it because I had to in order to feel good. This was not normal, but it became normal. I thought I was cool on the outside, but it was eating me alive on the inside. There were days that one led to two, and then I would end up drunk allllll day. This was an amazing experience, though I believe it just catapulted my drinking. I felt like I had let myself down. I obviously was not ready to be sober, I had zero tools at this time, and was not even close to 50% committed.

Life After the 99 Trip

I was biking and rollerblading to and from parties; I should be dead. This was an attempt to be safer than getting behind the wheel of my car while intoxicated--at least that is what I thought at the time. It was safer for other vehicles but not for myself. I was pretty good at getting around, just that when I would be so messed up, I had issues. It was dark, I was inebriated and putting those two together was a recipe for disaster. I cannot tell you the amount of rollerblading spills I had. I cannot tell you the amount of "near misses" I had. There were at least 5 times that I could not even walk my bike without falling over it. I remember one 4th of July a coworker saw me not being able to move the bike 10 feet without me falling onto it. He stopped and put it into the back of his pickup and gave me a ride home. I didn't even remember this until he

55

asked if I was okay the next day at work. He asked if I remembered anything, to which I replied that I did not remember how I got home. I thought maybe I had a dream that I saw him, but the reality is that he might have saved my life and I did not realize it at the time. I was pretty embarrassed and ashamed, but I did thank him and assured him I would not attempt anything like this again. I was so ashamed I wanted to quit my job of 6 years. Facing him and others was rough, though I was super grateful for his help. I was walking around on eggshells, embarrassed and ashamed. I remained quiet and avoided everybody at work. Well, that did not last long; how would I go from point to point be and still drink like I wanted to?

Chapter 9
Three DUIs in Hit-and-Run Accidents

Over the course of 20 years I was caught 3 times for hit and run accidents and for being under the influence of alcohol and drugs. Each time I came up with some sorry ass story to the police that it was not me that was driving my car, and that my car "Must have been stolen." I always flew the scene in hopes of not getting caught. I thought it wouldn't happen to me again—that I was just careless and had bad luck. I was both arrogant and reckless.

"I was glad to have been caught...but I still was not ready to change."

Each time I knew that I deserved the punishment, I was remorseful and glad to have been caught. Yes, glad. Glad because I thought these penalties and punishments would help get me sober. Even when I went to mandatory outpatient treatment, after a week of classes I started to drink after class and I did not take it seriously. I guess I was still not ready to change, thought the classes were a joke, and did not want to be there- just like high school and college. In fact, I remember not being able to wait until each class would end so I could go drinking. After hurting people, after totaling cars, after destruction of property, after heavy fines and lawyer's fees, it was still not enough to keep me sober for more than a few days.

Chapter 10

Culinary School, a Way Out of BD and Another Shot at Getting Sober

I worked at Becton Dickinson for more than eight years. I met some of the most wonderful people there and enjoyed working with them. They taught me a lot, and genuinely cared about me and tried giving me advice. They knew I had a problem and told me so, but it was up to me to change. I worked there longer than any other place. I put in a lot of hours, worked hard but really did not enjoy what I was doing. I struggled to find a real career. The only hobbies I had were partying, eating crap and sports. I was going to the gym regularly at this point, which was located next to my work. Drinking was my main career I wanted out! I started prepping food and bringing food from home to save money and eat healthier. I would marinate, cook and bring steak and chicken, make pasta, chicken parmesan, fresh fruit smoothies, and bring fresh fruit. My coworkers were constantly saying that they love the smell and kept asking if they could try some. So, I ended up making extra to share and it was costing me more money than before when I was eating out!

People were saying that I had real talent and said my food was really, really good. A few of them kept saying that I should sign up for culinary school. After hearing that over and over again, I said something along the lines of, "Fine, I will sign up if you stop nagging me!" It did really hit home. People really enjoyed my food and that is what the culinary industry is about. Serving great food and watching people enjoy it. I saw that there was a culinary school that was exclusively culinary in Cambridge, Massachusetts about 7 miles from where I lived. I decided to at least investigate what the application process was like. I drove down there and went inside and talked to them and picked up an application, and a loan application. This was in 2003 and I did not even have an email account or know how to use the internet. Well, this was it, this what I needed. I needed a change, I needed to make more money. Money would buy happiness, and this change was going to get me sober. I would focus all my time on culinary school and would not even have time for drinking. I was going to apply, get accepted and study hard, do well, and be sober. I knew that it was going to be hard to hold a full-time job, go to school full time, study and thought that I would not have the time party.

Well, addicts and alcoholics find time, and there is always a way! I could not stay sober, thought I would consume less alcohol on weekdays because I had less time, but I would speed up the process to get messed up by drinking more hard liquor and smoking more weed. Something had to suffer, and it was my work at BD. I would go to work really tired from school but extra tired from boozing and lack of sleep. I did really well at school and that is what my focus was. That was my priority because graduating held the key to happiness and a better life. I did not realize many things at the time and had a lot of false hope. I thought I would land a well paying job right out of school and did not think I would have to work my way up. Thankfully a few colleagues relayed this to me halfway through the program, and I was encouraged to gain employment in the culinary field to apply. Which I did, and I accepted a job at an assisted living home as a cook. I was happy and mostly sober for

59

about a week, and this novelty wore off and I started boozing hard again.

CSCA Culinary School

I really thoroughly enjoyed culinary school. I attended the Cambridge School of Culinary Arts in Cambridge, MA. Part of my addictive personality sidekick is OCD and all or nothing. I am all in, or nor vested at all. I fully embraced culinary school and I have to admit, it was pretty difficult coming from someone who was not book smart or did not like to study. But, I was all in and interested in learning everything about food and the industry and I studied and tried very hard. Unlike college, I paid for this myself and was really interested in the subject, so I applied myself. I did really well but really spent a ton of time going over and over my notes. For once I had a goal, a mission, a purpose. To do well, to graduate, to become a chef and make something of my screwed-up life.

During school I came down with a mysterious illness which was basically a pinched nerve in my triceps, which caused my right arm (dominant arm) to become limp and numb. A lot of cooking is hands-on! How the hell was I going to get by in culinary school with one friggin arm? I started thinking it through. I could stir, use tongs, slice, dice, but not easily. I started using my left hand, but it is not easy to say the least. I could not fold a puff pastry. It was difficult to lift or carry items; I could not do a lot of things. So of course, this was super stressful, and I drank a lot. I was so bummed out; my dreams were shattered. Something I actually loved was going to be taken away from me and it was not my fault! I was very angry and sad. How could this be happening to me? This made me drink more, that is what I did, I blamed this for my drinking. The correct answer was that I drank because I am an alcoholic.

I could write with my left hand, but by no stretch of the imagination could I read it or keep up with the lecture. I had a terrible memory due to years of alcohol and drug abuse and could not remember half the stuff unless I wrote it down! Thankfully I had some cool classmates and the chefs were very understanding. I was basically ready to take the second half of school off and re-register, but they let me slide due to my condition.

Culinary Career

After a stint at the assisted living home, I needed out of that place! Most kitchens are crazy and dysfunctional, and that place was no different. I started looking elsewhere. At this point I was growing tired of weed as it was just making me forget things. I was in the culinary field before BD, but now it was different. I needed my brain to learn as much as possible as I was not a teenager anymore. I accepted a position as a line cook at a restaurant. I really did not enjoy this from the start. I worked nights, though I am not a night owl and also it was interfering with drinking. I never really got the speed and accuracy of this position. It was really hard for me to time everything just right and keep up with the tickets that never stopped coming. I was totally overwhelmed. I wanted out of there after 5 minutes of my first shift. I remember I was reading Anthony Bourdain's *Kitchen Confidential* sitting in my car before work and

61

could relate first- hand as to what the book was talking about. I was living and surrounded by functional drunks and addicts who were lying, cheating, and stealing their way through the night, and life! I fit right in. This put me a little at ease as I was quickly realizing that the culinary industry was infested with alcoholics and addicts. I felt like this was my lifestyle and destiny after all... If you think you are messed up, look around! I was trying to get out of this life and quickly realized that a large percentage of people there and in the industry were like me, or worse. What am I getting myself into? Some were older, and fell accustomed to this lifestyle, or never had the courage or strength to seek help. Either they really enjoyed it, or they were stuck. I was amazed at how they could function AFUd. I could not! Some would be drinking and drugging on the job, I could not because it was really obvious when I drank. I stunk, and I was loud!

While working there, I had another run in with the law, after a run in with a telephone pole. This was the third of my hit and run DUI's. I was still in culinary school, working at the restaurant and had Sundays off. This was particularly great during football season because I could drink like I wanted to and did not have to work on Sundays, or Mondays and did not have to go to school until 3:00. Like I mentioned previously, the local sports bar that I frequented was where we watched football, drank beer and would duck out to burn a joint or two. We had watched both the 1:00 games and 4:00 games and a buddy of mine asked me if I wanted to come over for dinner and have a few beers and watch the evening game, in which I obliged. I recall smoking weed all the way there, well for 10 minutes or so and my other friend was following me in his car. I took the corner on to the friend's street perhaps too fast and eventually hit a telephone pole head on. I immediately got out of my car and a few women asked if I was okay, to which I replied "Yes, why?" Seconds later, I bolted on after telling my other friend that I would call him and have him pick me up. I ran basically about three miles through neighborhoods which seemed like an hour, then called my friend. He asked what I was going to do, and I told him to pick me up and drop me off at my house.

I got a call from the police at my parents' house and they asked to speak to me. I pretended that I just woke up and I was surprised that they were calling me, and when they told me what had happened, I told them I had no idea what happened--that my car must have been stolen. They asked if I had been drinking and I said, yes, at the bar down the street. They proceeded to go there and interviewed the bartender, the manager and also had the statement from the women at the scene of the accident. It was obvious that I was lying, and I went down to the police department to fess up first thing the next morning. This time was it; I was ashamed and done with drinking for good. I hit rock bottom I was ready to change--or so I thought. I honestly believed that I was ready at that time. Then, after a few days it changed to a different plan. I would just cut down, and from now on when I drank, I would limit myself to only having a few. This can work for a few occasions, but it's not sustainable if you are an alcoholic! I thought since I fled the scene I would just get a slap on the wrist and pay the fine. I didn't think I would lose my license. My case in court lasted almost 8 months which I will go into detail about later.

"No words can tell of the loneliness and despair I found in that bitter morass of self-pity. Quicksand stretched around me in all directions. I had met my match. I had been overwhelmed. Alcohol was my master."

Alcoholics Anonymous

Weed Really Stopped Working for me

They don't call it dope for no reason. I was tired of forgetting things, people's names, stories, really everything. It actually stopped relaxing me too. It ran its course and was not my real problem, alcohol was. They say that it is not addictive, I will disagree with that statement. There were a few years that I would not go to the gym, to work, rollerblade, a party if I did not have it. I had it most of the time but still, I feel like I was certainly dependent on it. On another note, I thought about using it to taper off alcohol once I started treatment, but I feel that the marijuana plan is not technically being sober. Any mind-altering drugs are not considered to be abstinent. I wanted to be 100% sober. I know people that did and still do use marijuana, I feel like it is still better than alcohol and if it helps them remain sober then more power to them; it is just not for me.

Chapter 11

<u>Move to Arizona; Running Away?</u>

So as this story goes, I had a job as a Food Stylist which is the coolest job I've ever had. I only had this job for six months. I was taught how to style food and got to play around with food. I learned that you eat with your eyes, and if it looks great then it tastes great. We made great food look great! And we got to eat most things; that was a bonus. And just like anything that was new to me it was a chance to get sober, at least temporarily. I really thought this job would change me and keep me sober. I was pretty lucky to have this job and was not going to blow it by drinking and under-performing. When I wasn't drinking that much I did well. When I drank in excess I did poorly. I wanted to move out of my parents' house in the worst way. I needed my own place and space. I looked for and went through the painful process of buying a condo. I did not have much money, but I was desperate to have my own place. I was forcing everything and completely distracted by the process. Honestly, I was stressed to the max combining that with drinking. No wonder I couldn't think clearly. I was a lost soul depressed, anxious, angry, and bitter. I would try and control or suppress all those feelings but the only way I really knew how to deal with them was by drinking like a fish. I would be shaky and unstable and quite frankly not the best employee or person at work that I could be. And it showed. I knew that if I wanted to do well and I wanted to keep that job I would have to quit drinking but I couldn't. I still wasn't ready in my mind. I wanted to stop but I just couldn't.

I also went through a really tough stretch here. Even though I was getting so messed up I could not really sleep at night so that I'm going to work super tired too. My mind was not able to rest; I was going insane. I was restless and couldn't shut my brain off and they were not positive thoughts--they were all negative. Just about every day after work I would continue to go to the liquor store and get what I needed to get through the day and night. I would wake up every morning, brush my teeth five times and drink like two gallons of coffee and hope for the best. I would walk around on eggshells the first hour hoping that someone didn't smell me or confront me. I worked with one other guy who was my mentor and my boss. I know he always knew what was going on; of course I tried to hide it and I'm sure I looked pretty shady. How much longer could I go on like this? I was just trying to live my life at that time like an alcoholic would and recover my behavior one day at a time. My goal was to get through each task, get through the morning, get to lunch, get to the afternoon, go home, stop at the store and then start drinking like I wanted to.

"My life was consumed by alcohol…I needed to find a way out"
I found my way to the store just about every day after work. I spent my workdays thinking about how I was going to drink and how much time I had to drink too. My life was consumed by alcohol. It kept me up at night and I needed to find a way out of this. I still lived with my parents, I wasn't happy, but how could I change my life? I didn't have money I didn't have a plan and I was becoming hopeless. I truly believe that everything happens for a reason and things happen not necessarily when you want them to. It is not always what Henry wants, and not always on Henry's terms.

One of my best buddies Jeff, whom I went around the United States with in the RV asked me if I wanted to go on a golf weekend in Arizona. He had a friend who had a timeshare condo and they were going to see the New England Patriots play the Arizona Cardinals. He asked me if I wanted to go. I always wanted to move to the west coast and I do like travelling so I thought about it and put in a time off request at work. It was September 2004 and I had not had a vacation since 1999 when I traveled out of New England. That was more than five years and exactly what I needed. I started thinking a little bit more about what it would be like to live in Arizona and always wanted to move to the west coast but I knew that California would be too expensive. What about Arizona? So I started doing some research on the internet looking for work. What's the cost of living among other things and kind of imagine myself living out there. It all made sense to me. I got the time off and decided to go on the trip. It was really all I could think about from the time I committed to going, I could not wait to get on the plane and fly out west! Waiting for the trip I still drank like a fish to pass the time. I was so excited by the possibility of finding a way to change my life. As the saying goes I partied like it was 1999 from the moment I left my house to get to the airport, at the airport, on the plane and then once we arrived and connected with everybody else the party continued. In fact, the party continued the whole time I was there.

Leading up to the trip I started looking for information online and I kept getting emails from Yahoo finance, Yahoo sports, Yahoo groups, Yahoo chat, and Yahoo personals. I never really looked at any of these except for Yahoo sports fantasy baseball and football. I didn't even know what yet what personals were until one day this subject was "Meet singles in your area just like you." And then it hit me. Why don't I try to meet a single in an area like Arizona? I believe this was meant to be so I created a profile and started reaching out to women in Arizona. I basically said that I was a chef that was relocating to Arizona and looking to meet women with similar interests and that I was going to be coming out to see if I liked it and wanted to connect with some women while I was there. And that's what I did. I had a few responses, one woman in particular became my long distance kind of girlfriend. We exchanged many emails and talked on the phone multiple times a day for about a month leading up to my trip. She was kind of all I could think about, along with the trip in general. I could not wait to meet her in person. I didn't have access to the internet during the trip so at that point I was committed just meeting her and didn't look at any emails or wasn't really interested in anybody else because we were so compatible, and I didn't want to ruin a good thing. I felt like if I did I was cheating!

So, once I got settled in, I hung out with my friends and drank like a fish at the resort. We went to the Patriots game at Sun Devil Stadium and they don't call it that for no reason; it was freaking hot in there. We had a really good time but it was between 200 and 203 degrees outside and I was drinking my face off. I ended up with sun poisoning and probably alcohol poisoning as well. My friends left for Boston the next day or the day after--I don't remember, and then I stayed an extra week. I had a hotel room to myself and was going to explore apartments, possibly look into purchasing a condo or something, look for work and just explore the area to see if I could live here. I arrived at the hotel and drank to get rid of the nasty hangover I thought I had but more than likely it was sun poisoning and alcohol poisoning. I really did not feel good and ended up not communicating with anybody including that woman for 2 days. I was very shaky and weak and couldn't eat anything. I didn't want anybody to see me like that, especially her. Once I finally felt better, I reached out to her and a few other people for that matter. I told her that my cell phone wouldn't charge or something like that. I don't know; I'm not much of a liar but I can't say that I told her the truth.

So, this woman came to my hotel room to pick me up and then we went and got some breakfast. After 5 or 10 minutes I had this awful feeling I didn't want to be there. I didn't want to be with her. We had already talked about everything and there was really nothing to talk about once we met face-to-face; it was so weird. We hung out for an hour or two after eating and that was the last time I talked to her. I was super disappointed and sad because I thought she was the one for me.

My buddy Cliff moved to Arizona three or four years prior to my trip from Waltham. It's not that I wasn't friends with them there, just that we had our differences. I was hesitant to reach out to him. I was not convinced he wanted to see me and I wasn't sure if I wanted to see him. But he ended up being super hospitable and inviting. In fact he insisted that I check out of the hotel they had for the week and stay with him instead. I didn't want to impose but I also wasn't sure if I was going to be able to drink like I wanted to do if I went to his place. I decided to go to his house anyway. I was happy to see him ask him what happened to him? He said, "Well I

69

have a 3 year-old, a newborn and a minivan, I've been domesticated!" I thought how cool is that? People can change. It was so nice to see him happy.

He picked me up and brought me to his house and after getting settled in and said "come on let's go outside, I'll fire up the grill and we'll have a few beers." I told them I really didn't want to go outside anymore and that I was kind of bummed out, and that it's too bad because this Arizona place is beautiful and really nice. I love everything about it. And that I would and could live here if it wasn't for the freaking heat. It's just too damn hot; every time I go outside I feel like I'm cooking myself probably because I am. He asked what I had been doing and I told him pretty much outside drinking. So, what the hell are you doing under the sun? He said come on let's go over and sit in the shade, have a few beers, have a few bratwurst, burgers and dogs. I remember it being 98 degrees. There was a slight desert breeze and we sat in the shade and just had a few beers and ate and talked for three or four hours and said I can get into this! At that point I had some sort of a spiritual awakening. My intuition was telling me to move! At this point I pretty much decided to move to Arizona. Thank you Cliff for inviting me over to your house, you helped influence the decision to move to Arizona.

When I returned home, I was both happy and sad. Happy that I ended up having a great trip after all, and that it appeared I finally found something positive that possibly could happen. I could move to Arizona if I wanted to. What's stopping me? Nothing is stopping me. The only thing that is stopping me is me. I always believed

70

that you can pretty much do everything you would like to if you put your mind to it. When I returned people asked me how my trip was. I said that Arizona's was really great; just that it was waaaaay toooooo hot, and at that point I didn't say anything about moving. I started getting a little bit of cold feet while listening to the voices inside my head telling me I can't move; how am I going to pull that off? I remember going downstairs to the basement where the computer was and logged on to check emails. I had quite a few of them including a few from Yahoo personals. I started to beat myself up for not at least exploring some other connections, and more of Arizona in general, but you can't take back time. A couple of women reached out to me and they didn't seem like a good fit so I just deleted those. And then there is one that stood out in particular. The email was a very well-thought-out articulate thoughtful email that was about five paragraphs long. It was from a woman who just moved into an apartment after starting a new job. She said she was sorry that we didn't connect. She was busy with the move getting set up and settling into a new job and apartment. She was hoping to be my tour guide and show me around the city and take me to a few good places to get some good food knowing that I was a chef. I sat there and looked at that email for about 25-30 minutes. I was kind of blown away by her kindness.

"I was my own support system and I sucked at it."

It took me about two hours, but I typed up an email message back to her, thanked her and told her that I was still thinking about moving because I hadn't committed at that point; I enjoyed it out there in Phoenix and wish we had connected. I apologized for not having any internet but so be it-- here we are. I have what I called at the time a new friend. I sent off that email and I waited near the

71

computer for 3 hours until I got a response! I started getting nervous and worried like, why didn't she reply yet after 45 minutes! She finally replied; we exchanged emails back and forth for 3 days. There was a 3-hour difference with the time zones which proved difficult for me, because I had to stay sober longer and later. This was much too late for me as I usually was well into my drinking and I didn't want to sound like a fool to her. At this point in my life, I had no support system. I had no sober friends. My family had their own issues with alcohol, so they were not too helpful. I was my own support system and I sucked at it. I was supporting my alcoholism.

It was pretty cool because I would stay sober long enough in the days after that so that I could read and reply to the emails with somewhat of a clear head. For the first time in a while I had some clarity. I had something to look forward to as well. She asked me to call her around 6 p.m. her time which is 9:00pm EST on Tuesday. I was a little bit nervous. I didn't want to screw things up. We hit it off. It was like we knew each other for years almost kind of hard to explain. I didn't want the phone conversation to end, but I knew there would be other calls and more. This was just the beginning. After talking to her I told her that I was 99% sure that I was moving to Arizona and actually meeting her online certainly helped my decision. After a few days of conversation and emails, later that week I decided to move. I could not wait to tell her, and next thing I knew, we were starting to make plans. It was difficult from 2800 miles away. With a 3- hour time zone change I had to hide who I was and hide the baggage and the drinking, but I think I managed to do so--at least over the phone and email. I wanted to change, and I didn't want to show her the monster that I was, which was an alcoholic and addict. I felt that this is what I needed. A woman in my life that cared about me, helped me grow as a human, helped me change my behavior. I felt that I could quit drinking. It was around somebody like her. This woman was Alejandra, who later became my wife!

Ironically, I lost my food styling job a week or so later. I think my problems finally caught up to me. I was told that I just wasn't getting it and they didn't understand why not. They didn't understand why my work is both so great and so poor and inconsistent and there were some things I just couldn't learn. They said it's time to sever ties and that was it. Forced change. I was pretty bummed out and angry about it because I really liked that job and I really needed a job until I moved. It wasn't the end of the world. I basically took what money I had and paid off my car, credit cards and then started putting together a solid plan to actually move in mid to late November. I had one more court date to find out my fate for the last hit and run accident that I had. In my mind since I just fled the scene so that I wouldn't get caught I thought that I would just get a slap on the wrist, pay a fine and be on my way. In fact, I had waived my right to a lawyer and decided to defend myself. I went to court and my case was brought to the table. The judge read me the riot act. She was so pissed off at me that I hadn't learned; this was the third time that I did this. I told her that I was going to alcoholics anonymous that I was going to change. I told her that I had not drank or been to a bar to drink since the accident. She basically said she didn't believe me, that I would lose my license for 60 days and I had to pay a large fine and court fees. I

73

would have to surrender my license the following day and that was devastating. This was going to screw up everything. This could screw up my relationship with my new long-distance girlfriend and the move to Arizona for sure.

This was not my fault; the stupid court system, stupid judge, what a bitch! Of course it was not my fault for drinking for 10 hours and getting behind the wheel of a car and speeding and hitting a tree. Well, I had to tell her. I told her that this was the truth and it happened in the past and found out I had my court date and sorry I didn't tell her earlier. I didn't tell her about my history of drinking. I said this was a one-time incident. I didn't want to lose her because she would be my reason to get sober. I told her I had morals and would never lie to her. This was certainly a red flag and a serious red mark against me, but what could I do? I had to fess up. I told her it happened earlier in the year, which was true--that I learned from it and that I don't drink and drive and don't really drink that much anymore. That was partially true. So, plans changed and instead of driving cross-country, I ended up flying out there on November 17th, 2004. Crazy thing about that date is that it ended up being my sobriety date later in 2008.

November 17th, 2004 The Move to Arizona

I flew out and Alejandra picked me up at the airport and it was love at first sight! Through the month and a half of phone calls and emails I felt like I knew her already but meeting her was super amazing. At that moment--even a little bit before that I kind of knew she was the one for me, and she was a good one. We both

74

enjoyed our first date here and celebrated my relocation to Arizona! Two days leading up to this I didn't drink anything. I went for dinner and I had two glasses of wine with her and thought that I could certainly moderate my drinking and only have a few. I was convinced of this. Convinced that being with a great woman would keep my drinking in check, and that she saved me. I know damn right well that an alcoholic cannot only have a few. As they say, one is too many, twenty is not enough; that's so true. I remember having a couple of beers the next night and she asked if I was drinking again. I told her that I was just getting settled in, and that it is kind of like I'm on vacation. And the next night I had a couple more. And the next night the same thing, and she asked me the same thing again. I said this was just a little phase. I was just trying to relax and enjoy my first week here. When we would get together with some of her friends or some of my friends, each time I got loaded. She was certainly upset and I'm sure she was concerned that I was not the person who she thought she knew. I told her I would stop and only have a couple of drinks a couple of times per week. That's kind of what I did for a while because I didn't want to lose her. I felt that if I did continue drinking, I would definitely lose her. I started ramping up my drinking again, testing the waters. I went through a whole spectrum of excuses as to why I was drinking. And she was on to me. It's cold out and I didn't realize it got cold in Arizona in November! It's warm, it's 85°. I'm drinking today because it's warm. Really, that was a reason! There's a basketball game on. The Coyotes are playing and the game is actually on TV; it's not subject to blackout. It's Sunday and it's football, I always drink all day on Sundays. Monday rolled around and I drank because I was sad that I couldn't find a job. Tuesday was a really good day, so guess what? I drink! Wednesday was a bad day. Thursday there's a good game on. Friday, hanging out with friends, I always drink with friends. Saturday, cookout=drinking. Football Sunday. Monday, rain so I am definitely drinking. Tuesday, another bad day, definitely drinking. The point is when she asked me why I was drinking I'd say there was a good game on, or it was cold, or I had a bad day. She didn't understand because everybody has good days bad days and there's always a game on; it doesn't mean you have to drink! I told her again that I was going through a phase and I was still kind of on vacation. I felt that I was pushing her away, so I cut down. I thought about quitting, but not yet, as I was nowhere near ready.

"We know that while the alcoholic keeps away from drink, as he may do for months or years, he reacts much like other men. We are equally positive that once he takes any alcohol whatsoever into his system, something happens, both in the bodily and mental sense, which makes it virtually impossible for him to stop."

Alcoholics Anonymous

My way has never worked, why would it start working now? As do many alcoholics and addicts, we try to cut down. We try to just drink wine, just drink beer, just have mixed drinks or just do a few shots. I tried everything. And eventually after just drinking wine I would drink two or three bottles of wine just to get the feeling that I was looking for and go back to drinking the way it was before. I was having a hard time looking for work. Actually, let me rephrase that; I was having a hard time finding a job. There are a million jobs out there and I applied all over the place, but I was getting zero phone calls and zero emails back. I started getting frustrated and funds were starting to get low. My Arizona vacation was almost over and I knew I needed to find work. I'd spend a couple hours a day every day networking and sending out emails, even knocking on doors. That's what I did in the morning until it was time to drink (11:00-Noon). I started drinking tequila and then I was drinking beer. The problem with tequila is that all of a sudden you go from 0 to 10 faster than you want to! I see now, I'm all fucked up! I remember being awakened by Alejandra while I was laying down on the kitchen floor of the house that we were living in. I had no idea how I got there, and it took me a little while to come to. I wasn't sure if I got tired, fell down and banged my head; I'm still not sure. But what I do know is that I was pretty messed up; it scared her and it scared me. Again, I said no more, no more drinking! That lasted a few days until the weekend came and I said I only have one or two. Now my drinking was being more scrutinized and watched. I was really under the microscope. We were having problems--all stemming from my behavior and alcohol consumption.

From 2004 to 2008 I think I went to urgent care five different times because of gastritis. The doctors there basically told me that I needed to stop drinking immediately or I could get stomach cancer, and that I was on the verge of severe liver and kidney damage. They would give me medication so that I could eat and medication for the heartburn. I wasn't eating healthy and I was drinking more than I was eating. And my organs took a beating. Each time I went and was diagnosed with gastritis or something else I vowed to quit

77

drinking forever. That's easy to do when you're vomiting and having diarrhea all day and all night and can't do anything about it. After going to the doctors, the meds kicked in and I was feeling better; then I would ease my way back into my drinking. I still felt like I could control it, and that the only reason why I got gastritis was because I wasn't eating healthy and drinking too much. I would start eating healthy for a little bit and cutting down on the drinking. I did reap the benefits of it; I felt better mentally and physically. But that was just a temporary solution.

"I was always thinking about the next drink"

While I was actually consuming the alcohol, the little devil inside me was always asking for more. I was always thinking about the next drink or if I could drink more or I wish I could drink more. If I had one or two early in the evening with dinner and had to sit there and watch everybody else drink, what fun is that? That's not fair? That's not fun either. After all, I was an alcoholic and I liked to get fucked up. I can barely get a buzz with one or two or three drinks because I had built up a tolerance, so it's just like a tease. So, the pattern continued. Whenever I got a chance to drink, I would say I only had like one or two. And again, my wife always knew I had more. We had countless arguments and problems over my drinking. It was just a vicious circle and cycle and always got worse.

At this point in my life I really didn't have any hobbies. I occasionally got the balls to put the roller blades on and take them out for a ride. But it was more of a joke than exercise. I fell down a few times and went nowhere near the distance I used to go when I lived in Boston, but at least I was doing something. We had two

78

dogs which was a nightmare at times. The dogs were supposed to keep me company so I wasn't lonely and hopefully I wouldn't drink as much. I would take them out for walks but nothing crazy either. I joined an LA Fitness and said that's it; this time the gym is going to keep me sober. I love the feeling of being in the gym, working out and the feeling after. It helps my confidence, my strength and my outlook in life. Three days later I found myself buying a six pack after the gym. Then that kind of became a routine. Get a killer workout and reward myself with beer. The concept is great! Except I was only lying to myself... The gym couldn't keep me from drinking. There's only two people that could keep me from drinking. God and myself. I didn't know that at the time. I thought I could keep myself from drinking, but I still didn't know how. The devil still had me in his grasp.

"Belief in the power of God, plus enough willingness, honesty and humility"

Alcoholics Anonymous

"I had trouble spending time with myself and was not comfortable in my own skin"

I remember Googling how to get sober without going to treatment. I was looking for some magic pill or something I could take every day to actually let me drink just less. There's shit like that out there but I know that's not the solution. It may or may not work and it's

79

just like a Band-Aid. What I didn't know is I needed to get to the source of the problem. I had trouble spending time with myself, and it was not yet comfortable in my own skin. Beer was my friend; tequila is my friend. As long as I had them around, I was entertained, I could silence my brain so that my feelings were warped and often suppressed. After a few days each time of cutting down or quitting that's when I realized and ran into difficulties. Spending time by myself and not being comfortable in my own skin was something I had a hard time doing.

Chapter 12
Marriage, Commitment Pact; Living in Hell Revisited:

Finally, Alejandra had had enough and asked if I would go to couples counseling. I believe I was like: "What for? Let's talk about this!"! She insisted, I obliged and we went to a woman that she had found online through insurance. It helped us but honestly, I felt attacked every time we went there. That's part of being an addict and an alcoholic, it's never our fault and everyone's out to get us. To this day, I still think she kind of favored my wife and didn't really listen to me. But maybe it was tough love too. She was a marriage counselor that specializes in couples with addiction issues. She certainly knew her stuff and insisted I went to AA meetings, which I did. I met some pretty cool people there, some old timers, got some good advice and heard a lot of things that I needed to hear. I was abstinent from alcohol and drugs for 60 days--somewhere around there and feeling okay. Physically better, mentally better, spiritually better. It was perfect timing, as I had this new-found clarity, I was presented with an opportunity that was too good to pass up. It was scary as hell, as I said no, I do not want to go initially.

Opportunity comes when you least expect it sometimes. My company received the exclusive catering contract for the 2008 Beijing Olympic games project. I was encouraged to apply on our website, as only 250 managers and chefs from around the world were going to be selected. This was a huge opportunity and I said, "What do I have to lose?" I applied. My wife is my biggest fan and really wanted me to apply. I think deep down inside she thought maybe this was my chance to show who I really was and a chance to get sober and stay sober. I had an extensive phone interview and was selected to be a chef for the 2008 Beijing Olympic Games! How crazy is that! They say in recovery that miracles do happen, and they happen often. This was a freaking miracle. But, when it came down to it I didn't want to go. I was scared and the reason I told my wife I didn't want to go was because it was 7,000 miles away, we are fourteen hours ahead in a different time zone and I didn't speak Chinese. It was pretty dysfunctional on my account and I couldn't imagine the dysfunction on an international level. I was overwhelmed with fear that I was going to be all alone over there.

I don't think I was very confident that I would succeed but deep down inside I think I was scared shitless that I would start drinking because I had more time on my hands. I always drank more when I had more time on my hands. For the first time ever I would be living alone--not with my parents and not with my wife. Subconsciously this was terrifying. I'm self- sufficient as far as cooking, cleaning laundry and errands and that type of stuff but could I take care of myself, could I stay in control enough in another country and another continent not to die, by drinking myself to death? Would I be able to do my job? I would be gone for four months. Four months. How could I stay sober for four months with all that time away from my wife? Well I couldn't. I was supposed to find AA meetings before I went out there which I did. I was supposed to locate them and actually go to them a couple times a week once I got out there, but I never did. I was concerned about staying sober for four months. I couldn't stay sober for four minutes once. What about staying in the moment? What about all the things I learned in AA?

Chapter 13
2008 Beijing Olympic Games Project

I got on the plane and a switch flipped. Before I even realized what was happening, I remember pressing the button to queue the flight attendant to come to my seat. When she arrived, my request was one mixed drink please? Then two, then three, then an hour later I arrived in San Francisco. A 1.5 hour flight! There I transferred planes and as soon as I got on the plane, one mixed drink, two mixed drinks, three mixed drinks. Thirteen hours later I arrived at the Beijing airport. I had no idea where to get my luggage. I was a mess. I ended up following a couple of other Americans and got pretty lucky. I was pretty lost and still messed up. I remember having a headache, basically hungover from the plane ride. I remember Thomas picking me up. He had my name on a poster board on it and one with chef Bob's name and somebody else. Thomas gave us a ride to the hotel where we were staying. I remember going to the 7-Eleven across the street and then having a few drinks and then going to sleep. I called Alejandra the next morning, as it was nighttime for her. I lied to her and told her everything went well. I just kind of slept in the plane. Well, that's not really a lie. The lie was that I drank the whole time. Day one and two, she doesn't know I'm drinking. At least she doesn't say anything to me.

I still didn't need to check in with work yet until the next day. I met a few of my colleagues, had a few beers and then we went our separate ways that ended up with me drinking alone like I wanted to. I drank so much that I missed the morning meeting with the team. I was so upset with myself that I drank! And drank. And drank. Finally, people came to the door of my hotel room to check on me because they heard that I arrived. They knew I was there; they were just wondering why I didn't go to work for two days! I told them I had jet lag and just wasn't feeling good. Don't mind the 2 empty bottles of sake and the 30 empties that were sitting on the counter though, those weren't mine! The next morning, I must have brushed my teeth a hundred times and found my way to (MPC) the Main Press Center where we worked. We went over to IBC International Broadcasting Center and the two teams had a giant meeting. It was basically training and orientation. I was still pretty foggy and wasn't comprehending much, but it was cool to see the buildings and meet a bunch of new people. Other people's mentality was the same as mine; after work, let's party. I remember going out for drinks after work. I remember grabbing beers for the road. Road beers for the walk, or for the taxi ride. Beers for massages, beers for pedicure, beers everywhere we went. I had been going to the 7-Eleven and stocking up most days. I think we had an arranged dinner on about day 5. My boss did reprimand me and confronted me as to whether I really wanted to be there. I was given an ultimatum. This caught me off guard. I was enjoying myself but not applying myself. I did not have a good attitude or the right work ethic. Although I was pissed off, it woke me up. I knew I had to have more clarity going to work.

I had already spoken to my wife and she called again. I don't know if she missed me or was just checking up on me to see if I was fucked up or not. And I was messed up, surprise! She told me

85

right then and there that she was still seeing the same family counselor by herself, that she felt strong enough to make a decision that if I don't stop drinking when I get home and if I don't take it easy while I'm out there she was going to get her own apartment and we would be separated. I could kind of tell that she was serious this time. I basically said in not that many words that this is going to be my last run and I would be careful. I did know that this is a huge stepping-stone for my career, a huge opportunity to learn a lot from people around the world, to experience a different culture and that I was super lucky to even be invited to be one of these 250 managers in the Beijing Olympic Games. It was an honor to be selected, and that I would not embarrass myself or ruin this opportunity.

We had it really easy out there; everything was much, much cheaper than the United States, including beer. Basically, you get a liter of quality beer for $0.50 so money wasn't an issue and I had the time, That's kind of what everybody was doing for the most part. This was extremely volatile for me. I thought nothing of grabbing some beers, going for a taxi ride and would just tell the driver to drop me off wherever, grab more beers, then walk around and just explore. When I would hang out with people, all we pretty much did was drink. There were other fellow alcoholics that were out there, that were in the same boat that I was. They were not supposed to be drinking either. That justified it for me; they too were going to stop when they got back again, so let's enjoy the last ride. It doesn't mean I had to, but I did. I had a lot of fun out there but perhaps I didn't learn as much as I could have. I don't think anybody is on their A-game when they are actively abusing, drinking alcohol and doing drugs and then trying to be functional at work. There's no way. I'm sure my attitude wasn't great and I didn't have the work ethic that I would have if I was not drinking and not hungover. I had no clarity either.

Beijing 12 Pack, Liters of Beer

So the Beijing 12-pack was something that I created. You could get a beer for like $.25 cents a draft beer at the Olympic venues and they would say, "How many?" I'd say "Twelve!" "Twelve?" "Twelve beers; yes, can I get twelve beers?" Sure. Okay then I'll have 12 beers. They would come back with some sort of box that they cut with twelve cups of beer. Thank you! That was kind of hard to carry so it was dirt cheap and the idea was to give them out to people I didn't know. I made new friends in the crowd! I would bring back two for my friends, keep three or four for myself and pass the rest out. And as you can imagine the second, third and fourth time I would do this I would be a little bit sloppier and would get the beer all over others and myself. I felt like a king being able to buy this many beers and just being able to pass them out. I would go from a king to a sloppy loudmouth rather quickly though. I remember one of the executive chefs had told me that it's not a good look to always have a beer. I would seem to bump into him everywhere. Perhaps he was meant to carry a message to me from God. He said every time he sees me I have a cup or bottle in my hand. I was a little bit annoyed, but I'll never forget that. You know that one guy or that one girl that is always drinking? Yeah, well they definitely have a problem--and so did I. I resented his comments at the time, but I respected it too. I think the first time I

87

saw him after he said that I saw him coming so I downed my beer! That didn't mean I didn't have alcohol on my breath. That doesn't mean that I wasn't messed up. I left a bad first impression. I felt he was out to get me; that is an addict's mentality.

All and all, no regrets, I did learn a lot and met some pretty amazing people, too. I got to see eight different Olympic Games from up close, including Michael Phelps winning a gold medal twice. I saw the men's Olympic Baseball team. I saw Bolt win gold. As my days in Beijing were winding down, I started thinking about coming home and how that was going to feel. I had a feeling of relief when it was almost over. I really and truly missed my wife and I missed being on American soil. I missed my favorite foods, I missed my dog, I missed our home, I was just tired of being away. I had a 60-day period of sobriety and I started thinking about what that was going to feel like when I got home. I knew what I had to do. Stay sober. Forever. This time I got this!

I didn't drink on the flight or the ride home as I knew I should not show up with alcohol on my breath, as my wife was going to pick me up from the airport. It really felt so good to see her and so good to be home. I had a brand new job as an executive chef at ASU poly campus. I was anxious, nervous but excited to be starting a new adventure there. And everything was good--actually everything was great. We celebrated being home by going to Rocky Point (Puerto Penasco) in Mexico which is a 3.5 hour drive to the closest beach from us. I had a great time, and for about a month I had this pink cloud. I had this feeling of euphoria that everything was great. Sobriety was going to be the new me forever.

But unfortunately, not yet. I had not learned the skills, and I was not 100% committed to sobriety.

My company invited all the managers in the United States for a dinner in Orlando, Florida to thank us for all the hard work and dedication that we did for the Olympic project. Basically, they flew us out there, put us in a hotel and held a commemorative dinner for us. My wife, who did not travel much for work, also was ironically traveling to Orlando! She was going to be there for I believe four days and three nights. I was just there for fourteen hours. You'll never guess what I did as soon as I got to the airport? Yep, you guessed it. I started drinking. I drank there and then I drank until they shut me off on the plane. What the fuck is wrong with me! Why did I give up on my sobriety? Why? Because I'm an alcoholic. During the thirty days of being back I was going to AA but I was lying to myself and I was lying to them. I didn't have all the tools. More importantly I wasn't ready to be done. I was not 100% committed to sobriety. I may have been 90%, I may have been 99%, but I was not 100%. It was like a switch was flipped with me. I don't remember even thinking about drinking until I got to the airport and sat down at a restaurant. Can I get you something to drink? Then it hit me like: "My wife will never know!" This will be my last hurrah. She would never know. Shit, she always knew. I felt that I can keep this one from her though, as it would be hours before I would talk to her.

I remember passing out on the plane and waking up in Florida! I don't remember taking a taxi to the location, but I must have gotten there somehow. I remember checking in and then meeting up with

89

my colleagues and then having a few drinks. I remember going into this dinner and it was an open bar, so I had at least two drinks going at once, and we did shots, too. Lots of shots. I remember being able to pass the first field sobriety test from my wife when she called me. Since she was now in Orlando, she wanted to meet up. I told her we didn't have dinner yet and I wasn't sure what the agenda was, but I knew that we'd be there at least 3 hours. She called me again an hour and a half later and I was kind of repeating myself. She then started interrogating me to see if I was drinking and she knew I was. She said not to call her anymore, not to text her either and that we would talk about it when we got home. She told me that I had an ultimatum--she was ready to move out if I started drinking, and I started drinking so that was what she was going to do. Every time I called her and texted her, I got madder because she wasn't picking up. She turned her phone off and I must have left her a hundred voicemails and texted her twenty times. Each time I texted or called her I got angrier--and of course it was her fault! Why couldn't she give me one more chance? She gave me 1,786,210 chances. Why didn't I deserve one more? And honestly, I got one more chance and I wasn't about to squander it and throw away everything. I knew I didn't want to lose her, and I knew I truly wanted to change.

So, after stepping out of the dinner one hundred times to text call and basically harass her, I was making myself angrier and angrier and continuing to drink more and more to ease the pain. My behavior was embarrassing to say the least. I didn't realize who I was sitting with at the dinner party. It was the President of Higher Education with my company, The Vice President, Director of

Human Resources and a bunch of other higher executives. God only knows what I said and only knows what I talked about, but I felt that they were ignoring me--which they should have. The highlight, rather the low light of the night was going on stage once they called my name to accept an award. I proceeded to the stage, which was where I took my shirt off to show everybody my Olympic tattoos on my back because I felt they needed to see it. I totally embarrassed myself but at the time I thought it was the height of the party. I did get quite a reaction when I went back to my table. I got some odd looks, too. I vaguely remember doing this to begin with and was reminded what happened afterwards. I was pretty ashamed. At the time I assumed I wasn't doing anything wrong, just being kind of funny or cool.

I was double fisted the rest that night, eventually went back to the hotel room and passed out, woke up the next morning, went to the airport and started drinking again. I drank on the plane and got home somehow-someway. A fourteen-hour bender with a little bit of sleep. Not that big of a deal. Well, as the fog started to somewhat clear I tried contacting my wife again but with no luck. I had this day off from work, so I went to the store and stocked up on booze. I purchased a 30-pack, tequila, rum and some junk food, probably some crackers and chips Doritos... I still felt messed up from the night before and the day before and so as soon as I started drinking, I was pretty messed up. I was also depressed, angry, sad, and quite frankly hating life. What was going to happen when my wife came home? Well she wasn't coming home for two more days, so guess what I did for two more days? Went to work, nope. Did the two-day cooking demonstration that I was supposed to do which was a huge responsibility? Nope. You'll never guess what I did. I drank and drank and drank; all I did was pretty much drink. I would fall down, I would black out and I would pass out and I would wake up and start drinking again. I didn't want to live. I wasn't suicidal but I certainly didn't want to live.

I was so messed up that I never called in sick to work. I just blew it off and blew off the cooking demos. I was so messed up I couldn't even use the telephone. I didn't want to talk to anybody, I didn't want to see anybody, I did not want anybody to see me the way I was either. I shut my phone off and I didn't look at the computer or anything. It was just me and Luci the dog and occasionally the TV. I kept throwing up and couldn't hold anything down. I started getting low on beers, so the next day so I staggered down the street and grabbed another 30-pack. That was a long walk to the store and certainly a long way back because it was heavy, and I remember falling all over the place. I struggled to keep consciousness; I had no energy because I just couldn't eat. The next day was the day before my wife was coming home.

Chapter 14
Rock Bottom
November 17, 2008 Time to Face My Demons, Head On

I became progressively worse. I knew I needed to go get some more beer for that day but I was really shaky. I had the cold sweats. I was planning on walking to the store, but I didn't feel well enough yet. So, I decided to take a nice shower and let the water hit me, help me sober up and get rid of the sweat. I remember sitting with my eyes closed in the shower holding onto the rail just praying to God that he would send me an angel to dispatch somebody to save me. I was really, really scared that I was going to die. I just kept blacking out and passing out and falling down. I begged God to send me anybody.

I had my clothes laid out on the bed waiting for me so after I dried off ,I put the towel down and walked out of the bathroom. There was a couple and a realtor standing there next to my clothes just staring at me with their jaws hitting the ground, and my mouth was wide open too as I was in shock. They were mortified at the sights they saw as I was completely embarrassed and ashamed of the condition I was in. I'm 99.9% this happened. Even if it didn't this was a sign or a spiritual awakening and quite frankly a miracle. They were my angels and God heard my prayers. They walked away. (We had put the house on the market because our adjustable rate mortgage went up and we could not afford it.) I got dressed, walked into the kitchen and proceeded to dump out my half drunk beer, then dumped out the three or four or whatever beers I had left, the tequila and the rum and any booze we had in the house. I threw

93

it out in the trash and that was it. I was done. I haven't touched a drop of alcohol since. November 17, 2008 is my sobriety birthday, anniversary. I was still pretty messed up and remember trying to force down some Cheez-Its and saltine crackers and probably some Doritos just to put something back in my system. I remember having a little moment of clarity that everything was going to be alright. A feeling of relief came over me. I was done drinking. I knew I still needed help because I was in rough shape and I knew I would need professional help, as well as a maintenance plan. I planned on going back to AA and knew I needed to get into some sort of treatment. I thought about a magic pill or something along those lines, but I knew I needed to do the self work.

The next day Alejandra came home. She came in with a suitcase and said we needed to talk. I was ready somewhat--ready to talk but not really ready to listen. At least I didn't want to hear what she had to say. She said that as I knew, when I was in China, she was seeing the same counselor that we saw and that she was strong enough to make a difficult decision now. She said she gave me an ultimatum and she was strong enough to back that up. She told me that while she was in Orlando, she secured an apartment for herself. I was in shock but what was I going to say? "Give me one more chance? I'll change, I'll go to treatment, I'll do anything?" Yeah, that's what I said. But she said she heard it all before too many times. I told her this time is different. I'm done. My word was not good enough anymore. She told me I needed to go to treatment right now or she was moving out. I told her I wasn't feeling well enough yet I was still really shaky, but I would go the next day. That's all I needed--just time to clear my head too, but I was definitely going to go. Well, she got the apartment. The next day I actually went to go <u>inquire</u> about treatment. I Googled a few places and found the one that I wanted to go to in Tempe which was close to where we lived.

"This went on endlessly, and I began to waken very early in the morning shaking violently. A tumbler full of gin followed by half a dozen bottles of beer would be required if I were to eat any breakfast. Nevertheless, I still thought I could control the situation, and there were periods of sobriety which renewed my wife's hope."

Alcoholics Anonymous

Chapter 15

I finally got the strength to leave the house and actually drive a car. I drove directly to Valley Hope of Tempe. I read up on it online and knew that they had an outpatient program there, and the other location in Chandler had inpatient one. I felt that I needed to still work for income, so outpatient was a better fit for me. I remember sitting in the parking lot for a few long minutes and then shutting the car off, opening the door, closing the door and feeling like this was a huge step. I remember then walking through the threshold to be greeted by a grizzly man with a bunch of tattoos looking like a biker. However, this man had 30 years sobriety and was a certified badass in life. He helped save my life. He greeted me with, "Can I help you?" I told him I was there to get some information about treatment and recovery. He said that he knew me. I don't think we met dude! He said I know you; you're an alcoholic and an addict. I said, "Well, probably." He asked me what I was really doing here. I said I came to get some information and I'm thinking about doing a treatment program. He said he would give me some information, "You're an asshole!" He was kind of out of his chair saying this too. I replied, "I'm an asshole?" "You don't really know me! Why are you so being so harsh to me?" He said, "You're an asshole if you came here to get information; did you come here to get help?" Well yeah. "Then why wouldn't you sign up?"

I told him I needed to get information. I had to figure out the money, how much insurance would pay, I had to talk to my wife. "So those are all excuses." I said, "Yeah they're good excuses but

96

they're all true". He said, "What lengths did you go to to drink alcohol and get into drugs? Any lengths?" Well, not any lengths but I did some extreme things. I thought of the rollerblading example in the rain to go by beer on a Sunday. He said, "What length are you willing to go to to be sober to get better, any lengths?" I said, "Well yeah any." "You said you want to be better, you want to be sober, you want to have clarity, feel better mentally physically, spiritually? Right?" He asked about my marriage and I told him it was in jeopardy. And he said, "What is the real reason you're here?" So, well, ummmmmm, my wife said she's going to leave me--at least to get her own apartment so I need to get her back because I really love her. He said, "That's bullshit." What? "That's bullshit." Okay? "If you want to get better you have to do it for yourself. " And you can't take care of yourself if you don't get better you can't take care of anyone else. You can't take care of a job." He said, "Your wife may or may not come back to you, but she certainly is not going to come back to you unless you get treatment or change right? If you can't take care of yourself you can't take care of your job, you can't take care of anybody else and you're probably not going to be married then why wouldn't you get help? The number one person in this world is you and it's your job to fix you. Nobody else's". He said, "We have the tools and resources here to guide you, but you have to do the work. Now what lengths are you willing to go to to get better? Are you willing to do treatment?" Well.. … yeah but…. "Then why not sign up?"

I basically said something like, "What's in it for you man, is this is some sort of business, do you get commission on this?" He said, "I don't get commission and I don't give a shit what you think. I just know that you said you'd be willing to go to any lengths to get help, when you came here looking for information. This place will give you information, but you need to register for the treatment. You need to go through the program." I said, "Well I have to figure out the money thing." He said, "That's bullshit, money doesn't matter." "You leave this place now and you go to a liquor store and you start drinking like a fish and die. Was the money really that important?" He said, "The time is now; today and tomorrow is not guaranteed. If you said you would go to any lengths to get better is money really that important? You can always make more money? It'll cost you a couple grand, is your life worth more than a couple grand? Think about how much money you've spent in the last month alone on beer, booze, drugs, cigarettes, whatever. Do the math. It's all pissed away and it's toxic. Treatment is priceless. Getting in a treatment is ultimately saving your life, if your life's not worth it then maybe this isn't for you."

"The first time I had confidence I could become and remain sober"

I said, "Fine, I'll sign up. I remember thinking to myself I'm going to sign up just to shut this guy up. I'll never see him again. I don't have to show up the next day. I didn't give any money yet. But I walked out of that door with a feeling of closure and a feeling the new chapter of my life was actually going to happen this time. The first time I ever actually had confidence that I could become and remain sober. Something else that he said really hit home. He said I can never drink or use ever again. And that was pretty powerful and powerful enough for me

by completely understanding that

"There I humbly offered myself to God, as I then understood Him, to do with me as He would. I placed myself unreservedly under His care and direction. I admitted for the first time that of myself I was nothing; that without Him I was lost. I ruthlessly faced my sins and became willing to have my new-found Friend take them away, root and branch. I have not had a drink since."

Alcoholics Anonymous

I immediately told my wife that I had enrolled into treatment. I had hoped that she would cancel the apartment and just come back home to our house. She said she had made her decision. Which was pretty confusing; we had a house to live in, I was going to change. I enrolled in treatment like I said I would do. I signed up for treatment, but she still was going to move to an apartment? How could I argue at this point? I needed to work on me, and if I worked on me. I had a chance of patching up my marriage in due time. My priority was working on me.

"Our behavior is as absurd and incomprehensible with respect to the first drink as that of an individual with a passion, say, for jay-walking. He gets a thrill out of skipping in front of fast-moving vehicles…he is slightly injured several times…after leaving the hospital…he tells you he has decided to stop jay-walking for good but in a few weeks he is hit and breaks both legs."

Alcoholics Anonymous

Alcoholics and addicts cause a lot of damage to themselves, to relationships, to situations and part of the process is to make amends and do some damage control. There was a lot of wreckage

99

behind me. Being accountable and fessing up to our wrongdoings is part of the healing process. I think it's important to try to do some damage control to clear the mind of guilt and try to repair relationships if it's deemed appropriate. Saying I'm sorry or taking ownership is humbling and part of the healing process. For some people and in some situations, I was not ready to take ownership or to even tell them that I was in treatment or to apologize yet, for that matter.

"I let my actions and my performance speak for who I was now"

One thing I needed to do was to make amends at work. I realized that I had a couple voicemails from my director wondering where the fuck I was for three days! I had at least two days with no call-no shows. I had to reach out to the company that I subcontracted for as well about the cooking demonstrations. I kind of thought I lost both gigs. I did not tell either of them the exact truth, but I did tell them that I had an emergency with my health. That was the truth. I stated that I had a life-threatening emergency that I need to take care of. A few more days the way I was going I could have died. I was in that rough of a shape. I believe this was my rock bottom. Looking back, if I had told my supervisors I was in treatment, they probably would have been supportive. The plain truth is, I was just too embarrassed. I did not lose either of my jobs. In fact, with both of them I was put on some sort of a second chance probation. I was a little nervous going back to my full-time job, but I had nothing to really be ashamed of or hide. I just needed to move forward. I was walking around on eggshells, but I knew that I had to move forward. And indeed, after a couple days I was fine. I became a solid employee, happy and productive. Nothing was ever said

Chapter 16
Now Back to My Marital Situation

I was feeling really good in general physically, and at work. I was very happy with my treatment, though I was just still screwed up about our marriage. I helped my Alejandra move everything she wanted to her apartment and made sure she was 100% situated. We were separated; however, I spent most nights over there! We eased our way back into our relationship while not skipping any steps. This was a chance to rebuild and start not from scratch, but we had new chapters to write. I still needed to repair the damage and regain the lost trust. I had this pink cloud feeling of euphoria from the clarity and the sobriety. I was happy most of the time but dealing with damage control forced me to tap into emotions that I was suppressing and drowning in alcohol. I was angry, sad, and depressed a lot of the time when I was drinking.

So, what was the source of the anger, sadness and depression I was trying to suppress with alcohol? Others had what I wanted, materially that is. I didn't know how to get it. I was jealous and at the same time, angry at myself for drinking and not changing to get better. When I got clarity, I realized they worked hard for what they got. Now that I was sober and had clarity, the sadness that I had sometimes felt different, and it was kind of weird because it had been a long time since I had to deal with it without alcohol. When I was angry it was the same thing. Instead of going to the bottle and drinking a bunch of beers, I had to deal with my problems head on. The treatment in the recovery process helped me deal with these properly. The counselors at Valley Hope gave me the tools and the knowledge. It is okay to be sad, it is okay to be mad. These are emotions and it is just how you choose to deal with them. But, after suppressing these emotions for 20 something odd years it was kind of weird and surreal to deal with them with a clear head. I was really confused about our marriage. Money was an issue. We were selling our house because our mortgage kept going up, up, and up and we could not afford it, and my wife got an apartment? I want to say the apartment was $1,200 a month. What was she crazy about getting an apartment? And then we have bills we can't pay on top of that? What the hell is she thinking? She was thinking that she needed security. She was thinking there is a really good chance that I was going to fall off the wagon, go back to my old ways and go back to the way I was before--drinking, negativity and further down the downward spiral. Those odds were great.

So, she protected herself, she stood her ground and secured the apartment. I had to accept that. Which, I had a hard time doing because we still had the house, debt, and I spent just about every night at her apartment. I spent a decent amount of time with her still, and we were separated? Figure me, but I think separated means apart, right? We were spending all this time together and sleeping in the same bed; that is not separation. WTF. I accepted it but I was confused. I did not fully understand where she was coming from and assumed that the lease was month to month. After 3 weeks of being there I asked her if she was going to move her stuff back to the house. She said no, that she had a lease and she would not tell me how long the lease was for. I assumed it was month by month. She finally told me that she signed the lease for a year. Oh my God, we have to live like this for a year or until we sell the house or what? Same thing, I could not worry about a year down the road. I could not live month by month; I need to work on being a better person day by day, moment by moment and stay in the moment. That was critical for my recovery and critical for my relationship with her. She did not grow up around a bunch of alcoholics or alcoholic abuse in general and really did not understand it.

At Valley Hope, Thursday nights were family nights. Significant others and family could be a wife, husband, children, boyfriend, girlfriend, or whoever; they are encouraged to come and participate, listen and learn what the recovery program was all about. It was a lot about them too and offered insight into Al-Anon. Al-Anon is specifically for family members that have addicts or alcoholics in their family and it helps them understand the disease. It helps them understand how to cope and helps them take care of themselves. Alejandra reluctantly came to family night but ended up fully embracing the program. She quickly started to understand what an alcoholic is and what it is like to be married to one. She did a lot of research like she always does and read a lot on the subject and quite often came on Thursday nights. She met some new friends and became somewhat of a leader in the discussions. She learned about enabling an alcoholic, tough love which she already knew from counseling, and how to move forward.

I told my mother about my large problem, how I was enrolled in treatment and that we were separated. I told three friends as well and they were kind enough to listen to me and respect me. I needed someone to talk to that cared and knew me, it helped me get what was bothering me off my mind without complaining. I felt they should know that I was changing and committed to this and was 100% accountable. I felt this would help with accountability. If I say I'm going to do something, I do it. I did talk to all of them about being separated and about our debt, why we were carrying extra debt, why my wife insisted on getting an apartment and why she got a one year lease! It was mind-boggling for everybody but what they did not fully understand was where she was coming from. Like I said before, she did it to protect herself and I completely understand now. At the time I did not understand, and it screwed me up. I decided to see a therapist myself.

I could write an entire book about my wife Alejandra. I tell people that she is the greatest person I have ever met, the most caring, and loving person in the world. She saved me, and it is possible that I would not be here without her, and without her love. I could go on and on about her, but I owe her my life because she helped save mine. I am very grateful for my mother's unconditional love too. She has put up with my crap for 50 years now and never gave up on me, even though I put her through hell, and she probably should have given up on me. This goes for the same with my sisters. I was not the best sibling, especially when we were in our 20's. Thank you for sticking it out and having faith in me!

Chapter 17

Therapy

I found a therapist that was fairly close to the house and after the first consultation I really felt it was a great fit. This guy kind of had an in-your-face persona just like the man who greeted me at Valley Hope. He was a funny guy and did not hold anything back, which I respect. We got along great. I was very open with him; I was there to get help and just an unbiased resource where somebody that did not really know me could give me an insight and guide me in the right direction. The main reason I went there is to understand where my wife was coming from. He helped me with that, and he helped with many other things that I really did not realize I needed help with. I was newly sober and started embracing life more. I as happier at work and at home. Miracles were happening and I did not want to lose that feeling. Most of all, I did not want to go back to the way I was before. I knew if I kept working hard on myself the universe would give me good things in life. It has a way of giving back to you if you create positive energy.

He told me after the first consultation that he thought that I was missing something in life. I had a void that needed to be filled. He asked me what I was missing in my life? I said that I did not know, but quite a few things. I had a career, I actually liked what I was doing at the time, I really did love my wife, I love my dog, we had a house, I now have my health and some clarity and the willingness to change. What else could I ask for and what was I missing? I always prayed for more money; maybe I was missing more money? It is common for people that are alcoholics and addicts to always want more, never being satisfied. We talk about being grateful and writing gratitude lists. I was grateful for all the things above and still am. What is missing? If I was happy and grateful for all those things and I do not need anything more than what am I missing? The only thing I could come up with was that other than my wife and my son, I had no outlet. I had no adrenaline rush.

It took a few more sessions for the stuff to really come out. It is not that I was not happy, but something was missing. Alejandra told me the same thing that he told me; I have a difficult time being in my own skin and spending time by myself. I have a difficult time sitting still. I told him and I told her that they were wrong. Over the years I spent a lot of time by myself being sad, lonely, depressed and angry. He said, "Yeah, that was before; that was before when you were drinking. You always had a friend, you had beer. Beer kept you company." Whether I like it or not it did. He was right. Beer helped entertain me. I need to be entertained. Since I was no longer drinking or thinking about drinking, I had more time on my hands. I would go over to my wife's apartment or she would come over to the house or we would go out to eat when she got out of work. I really was not spending that much time alone and when I did, I did not know what to do with myself. The house was clean for the most part. All my laundry was done, and I had groceries, I was eating and would spend time playing around on the internet. To actually spend time by myself, I did not know what to do.

He asked me what I used to like to do that really gave me a rush besides drinking. What put me in my happy place and what made me move? What lit my fire? I told him that I used to enjoy going on adventures on rollerblades and mountain biking. I loved feeling

110

the adrenaline rush when I was flying down a bike path or a hill and enjoyed going for walks. I told him I loved live music, listening to music and buying CDs. He said, "What the fuck? Why didn't you tell me this before?" Well, it never came up until you asked! He says "I've got it." I said, "Got what?" He said, "I figured out who you are. You're an adrenaline junkie." He said, "You do have trouble sitting still, you do have trouble spending time with yourself and you are not comfortable in your own skin so we will work on that--but you are an adrenaline junkie you need to do something. You need to move; you need to feel those endorphins. Why don't you ride your mountain bike?" Why don't you grab the rollerblades and strap them on?" "Well, I've done it so many times that I'm kind of tired of it." "It's hard to explain. I'm just kind of burnt out from it." "I need something different." He told me to try to do it to see how I felt--to see if it still had a spark and if it's still kind of ignited that fire. I tried it and it did, but it felt weird. I went rollerblading and I had this weird feeling. I couldn't figure out what it was at first. Holy shit! This was the first time that I ever rollerbladed without being high or having a few beers in me, at least a few! I didn't have that unstoppable feeling, that fearless feeling and really kind of had to think about what I was doing not just on instinct and balls. It was so weird; it's not like I had to reteach myself how to do it but I had to get in the right state of mind! But after ten or fifteen minutes I was fine and I actually enjoyed it. I did that once in a while and took the bike for a ride once in a while and it kind of helped. Going to this therapist once a week or every other week really helped me understand my relationship with my wife, her decision and it kind of gave me a better focus and perspective of who I was, where I wanted to go and how to get there.

111

Chapter 18

March, 2009

All and all I enjoyed my job as an Executive Chef and had a nice routine going at work. I was grateful for my job for the most part and with clarity, it became easy. It wasn't a very high- volume account and the only time I was really busy was when I had catering. I enjoy the hurry up and wait aspect of catering. You do all this prep work and then you fire the food, plate it up and present or serve it at the last minute. This got the endorphins kicking too and the heart rate up. The hard part is having all the food come out at the same time to the right doneness and temperature and serving it to the guests was right up my alley. But if we didn't have catering it was pretty routine. I was in charge of making two or three entrees, three different types of soups and I oversaw the staff of six. I did the Sysco food orders, inventory and other management duties, too. I was in charge of cleaning my area and planning for the next day. I took care of all the menus and helped with marketing too. I was willing to take on any new tasks and often offered help to others. I was on the verge of becoming complacent because this job became pretty routine. I was thinking about my treatment. I started thinking about my happiness. Was I happy there? Was I grateful? Was I now complacent? Was I overqualified? I needed to answer these questions. In retrospect, I think I was fine there, and I just know that I like to be challenged. It was challenging when we had catering because it was just me working on it for the most part. I still had to do my other duties, then do catering on top of that and the timing was always hard. I only had so much workspace, so much storage space and only so much space in the ovens. I always pulled it off; it was cool to try to

112

figure everything out and I often was running around. I started thinking about how long I would want to stay at that account, or if I wanted to move. Just as I started thinking that I wanted to stay my questions were answered for me.

I found out from my staff that this location goes to a skeleton crew in the summer because there's hardly anybody there taking courses. Meaning, they only need a cashier and someone else that did grill, deli, utilities and clean up. That was it, and that person would not be me. I was an Executive Chef and I would not be needed for at least two months. That meant I was going to be temporarily laid off. Hell yeah, I have the summer off! Well, only able to collect $240 a week? That was not an option. Money was still an issue and that would not be sustainable. I started networking with people that I met around the world in Beijing. I started asking around if anybody knew of any positions that might be available or any guidance as to what to do within my company. A mentor that I had when I first signed on with our company who actually invited me to apply for the Beijing Olympic project suggested that I look into the kindergarten-grade 12 line of business within our company. She said go on to the K-12 portal. They have applications for short-term assignments in different states. Our company was going after K-12 school contracts or rebids and needed support. I noticed that there were some opportunities in the state of Massachusetts, so I applied for the short-term assignment. It said in the description support is needed anywhere from one week to two months in some cases.

I filled out the application and a recruiter called me a few days later and we had a healthy discussion. She obviously had my resume, we talked about the Beijing Olympic Project, then onto my experience and also about my situation at work. I told her that I'd be interested in going to Massachusetts because that's where I grew up. I had family there and friends and mentioned that my sister was having her first child, plus that there were two weddings in the summer. It would be cool to be there for at least one of them and work at the same time! The discussion changed from short-term assignment to possible relocation! I had this immediate intuitive feeling that it was too good to be true. Possibly moving back to Boston? No, this is too good to be true. My wife and I had talked about starting a family and potentially doing that close to my family or her family. She and I visited Boston a few times, she sure likes it there and it was a possibility. This is another freaking miracle they talk about! But I still had that feeling that it was too good to be true. She talked about a relocation package. She talked about the salary range. This would be an Assistant Food Service Director/district chef position with a lot of opportunity for growth. I couldn't believe it. I had confidence but not that much, and certainly not to be an assistant food service director. Why would she even consider me? Why was I the best candidate for this position? The answer is that God felt I was ready. I assume she had not talked to the Director of Human Resources or the Vice President or the President of Higher Education!

I was excited but kind of convinced deep down inside that it wasn't going to happen. I learned in recovery to never get too high because you get bitch slapped down or never too low, to stay on an

114

even keel in the middle. So, I didn't jump to any conclusions and let things play out. I had a great discussion with my wife, we talked about it and what happens if they offer me a job. A week or so later I was offered the job! I spoke to my sister who was in human resources, we talked about the offer letter and she helped give me the confidence and courage to ask for more money--a signing bonus to go along with the relocation package which they offered me. Unbelievable! This was kind of a dream come true that I never saw coming. Everything happened so fast. I think this was in April and by late May I found myself driving across country with my dog Luci and with my clothes and things I would need to get started. I moved first. Alejandra wanted to make sure that I liked it out there and that it was the right decision. She stayed back and also finished up her job, which she really loved and was potentially going to leave behind. She moved in November. I'll talk about that a little later. I came out a few times that summer and I went back to Arizona a few times, too! Big move back to where I grew up and kind of where my heart was on my mind a lot. We were really excited about this opportunity career-wise, the new start and excited about being close to my family and friends and places in New England!

Chapter 19
<u>Move Back to Boston</u>

Moving back to Boston was another fresh start for my wife and me. It was cool in the beginning to have a different outlook and see things differently. I took things for granted growing up there, whether it was about how historic New England is and the beauty of it, or relationships with people. I had a whole new perspective thanks to clarity and being sober for eight months now. Interesting enough some places were the same and so were some of the people and friends that I used to hang out with. Some friends did change, but some are the same. I had a couple friends that I used to hang around with all the time that I saw shortly after arriving, and all three of them asked me at least once if I wanted a beer or to smoke a joint or smoke a bowl. At least once. And this is after I just finished telling them about my sobriety. It was Saturday morning, and they were already fucked up. In the past, that would have been me right there with him. Surely these are not friends that I would be hanging around with anymore. I enjoyed going to local restaurants, sub shops and pizza places that I used to frequent and seeing friends and family in general.

My new position at work was challenging and something I had never done before. K-12 is not as easy as it sounds; you have to please too many people. You have to please your company, the department of education, the city or town you work in, the teachers, the administration, the superintendent, the principals, the board of health, the union staff and then there's the students! There's a lot of rules that were challenging to learn. I spent the summer doing that and assisting with the summer feeding program. I quickly learned that my teacher, who was the Food Service Director, was a raging alcoholic and a chain smoker. He constantly repeated his stories, so after about a week and a half I knew all of them. We would go 2 miles down the road. It would take ten minutes in traffic and he would light one cigarette off of the other one, smoke at least two on the way there and two on the way back. Doing this twice I decided from now on I would just take my own car. Even though I smoked, it was disgusting and hard to watch! I felt bad for him and realized that this could possibly happen to me or any other addict. I feel like he had it bad. He was a very negative person and often talked about people. He was condescending. He came off really nice when he was speaking to the right people and often acted politically, but when you talk to him behind the scenes, he was a lot different. He was a narcissist. He was not a great teacher; he was old school and had no clue about how to use a computer and everything online. I found myself learning on my own and was grateful for the other Assistant Food Service Director Amanda. I learned to apply what I learned in treatment at work. I could not control how he acted or how he thought. I can only control how I thought and how I acted. I lived and worked in the moment and took care of what I needed to that day.

The novelty of being back home started to wear off. After a few months this pink cloud of being home and was dissipating. I wasn't sad or complacent or bored--just that something was missing. I still had this void. Some of the friends that I used to hang out with all the time, my core group of friends were still around. It was cool seeing them as everybody now had a family and kids. It's not that I

117

didn't have anything in common with them anymore, but it was just different. Something was missing in me. I still had no hobbies.

Chapter 20

Alejandra's Move to Boston November, 2009

After going back a few times to Arizona I flew back for the final
time there to tie up loose ends, help pack boxes, pack the car with
important stuff--including Alejandra. It was time for her to make
her move cross-country! We saw the movers off and we were on
our way. She was excited about the move but really didn't want to
leave the great job she had. It took a long time for her to let that go.
But she knew it was a huge career move for me, and again we
wanted to be close to my family. The first few months, I enjoyed
introducing her to more of my favorite spots and we did a lot of
road trips to different states in New England, and we also visited
our friends in New York. All and all we were enjoying ourselves
despite the long cold winters. But I still really had no hobbies. I
started walking on weekend mornings and occasionally
rollerbladed. Every year, my extended family organized a fall hike
in New Hampshire and was doing one again this year. Now that we
were living in Massachusetts, I told Alejandra I was going to do the
hike, and since I still smoked occasionally, she insisted that I get a
physical first, and said that I was out of shape. She had doubts that
I could do it and just wanted me to get checked out. She didn't
think I could do it. I told her I used to hike, that I was not that out
of shape I joked, but vowed to be the first one to get to the top. I'm
pretty competitive and did know I could do it. So, we went up to
New Hampshire for the weekend--cousins, aunts and uncles. Guess
what? I was the first one to the top! I felt pretty great once I
finished and couldn't wait to tell her. Not to rub it in her face, but
she never really saw the athletic side of me. I was not about to do

that because I really enjoyed the way it made me feel. I love adventures; you never know what you'll see. This hike lit my fire inside. I was sore the next day and obviously got a great workout. It left me wanting more as I wished I could have done that more often, but there are no mountains nearby where we lived in Belmont, Massachusetts. It's at sea level. Prospect hill is in Waltham but for me at the time it was a pain in the ass to get to because of traffic. It's something I could do on the weekends, but I wasn't able to do it by myself. Also, the weekends are for family time...

Chapter 21

Squirrelly: Running with a Squirrelly Devil

Since I was a kid I have had a hard time sitting still. I probably should have been diagnosed with ADHD, OCD, ABC, XYZ and everything else in between. The reality of it is I just need to keep busy because I have a lot of energy built up inside. I believe there is positive energy and negative energy. I had a lot of both, and I just didn't know what to do with it. I would drive myself nuts and drive my wife nuts, too. Saturday and Sunday mornings were the worst. My wife likes to sleep in and I would be up at 5:00 or 6:00 AM and going insane. The house would be clean, all my chores would be done and I had nothing to do. I was tired of the internet and didn't feel like watching TV or feel like reading. I was done with everything I wanted to do and was searching for something else, but what? Why do I have this void; what am I searching for? Am I comfortable in my own skin? Coffee certainly did not help much; it just made me more anxious, but I drank a ton of it. Now I know better! I was still having a hard time in my own skin apparently. Or was I? I don't know but I hate being indoors and I felt like going out. My mother had given me a GPS watch that I wanted, and I used to really start tracking how many walks I did, and the distances. I started walking more and walking became a self-challenge and I guess a hobby, I liked to see how many walks I could do in a week.

I started walking and I would walk a distance. I would grab our dog Luci and head out on a Saturday morning. Sometimes I would go as far as Harvard Square, which was two miles away, which meant I had to go two miles back, so a total of four miles. That is pretty far to walk! This would take between an hour to one hour and fifteen minutes. I would go to the Charles River which was a mile and a quarter from the house and walk along the river and the bike path. Sometimes I would bike ride into Boston, which was neat, too. We lived in a third floor apartment and Luci had gained some weight from a lack of walks, but once we started walking all the time and we put her on an ice cube and carrot snack diet, she dropped the weight. She was my training partner and my faithful companion, and she loved it too. There's so much to see for her from people on bikes to squirrels to pigeons! I gradually started increasing my miles and would say hey let's walk to Central Square, which was an extra mile or so from Harvard Square. I walked to my parents' house which was three miles away, for a total of six miles. They and other people couldn't believe how far I had walked. It started to become the weekend ritual and fairly routine. A bunch of times I was offered a ride home which I politely declined. I enjoyed many of the benefits of walking, from just being outside, to the exercise, to the adventure and the fact that I could disconnect for a while, which was huge for me. I could get out of my own head! I want to say the longest day I ever walked back then was somewhere around seven or eight miles. I would go through the whole spectrum that runners and endurance athletes go through. I would have a decent amount of miles to go, or I wasn't even at the halfway point and still had to come all the way home and swear I WOULD NEVER do it again. But as soon as I got home, I would start plotting my next route.

I was starting to fill a void, I was still looking for happiness, or something. I was missing something. I started buying more and more scratch off tickets but then I stopped for a while. I realized my actions were out of desperation and I was spending the little play money I had, and it was automatic. I would get paid, take out my play money and I developed a habit/ addiction of trying to get rich! I also realized I was trying to buy happiness, but I do now know that happiness comes from within. One million dollars would make me happy, but not for that long. I needed a better plan. I recognized I was trying to fill a void.

Chapter 22
Life Quickly Changed- Seven Dwarfs Motel New Hampshire
July, 2011

Speed up to July 2011. We had decided to take off for the weekend and go up to one of our favorite places, the White Mountains of New Hampshire. We decided to stay at a place near my friend Eric's old trailer called the Seven Dwarfs Motel. They had cute little cottages and homemade breakfast, literally homegrown. The eggs were from their chickens and the bacon was from their pigs. I didn't know this the first time I had their breakfast (pre-culinary school!) and knew it tasted different but it sure was extra delicious. We didn't spend much time there as we are usually on the go. We went to North Conway on a nice ride on the Kangamangus Highway, did some little nature walks along the way and went to some of our favorite places to eat. The Pemigewasset River ran behind the Seven Dwarfs motel and I remember Alejandra feeling kind of weird. She had her feet in the cold water, and she said she felt different. I asked her if she was okay; she said, yeah, she just felt weird! At night we went to one of my favorite places to go, the Woodstock Inn. They have great food and homebrews. Not that I drink anymore but Alejandra enjoyed one beer every now and then. We sat at the bar because there was no other space. We were lucky to get two seats together. We ordered a few appetizers and she drank a little of her beer as we waited for our dinner.

She turned and looked at me and said, "There's a chance I might be pregnant!" I'm like, yeah right okay. She said just in case I'm not going to drink anymore of my beer. My immediate reaction was , finish that, it costs like $6! And she said she hadn't had her period yet. She felt a little bit nauseous, and just couldn't really explain it but she felt like she was pregnant and wanted to go get a test kit. The next thing you know we drove a mile or so down the road to the Rite Aid and picked up a kit. We decided to wait until we got home to actually do the test but the remainder of that night and the next day, Sunday, were kind of weird. We started kind of bugging out a little bit and thinking about what if we are pregnant, what do we do? For the first time in our lives, we're actually just starting to try to get pregnant. They say you'll never be financially, spiritually, career-wise ready or all the above. If you keep waiting, it might not happen. There is no way she was going to have a kid with me the way things were going when I was drinking. There's no way we could have afforded to either. At this point in our marriage, we were stronger than we ever had been, and I was finally getting most of her trust back, and the timing is right, so we said, "Let's try." We enjoyed the rest of the weekend and then came home, and it was time to face the music. She went into the bathroom, performed the testing and came out and said, "Do you want to know?" I said something along the lines of, "Do I have a choice? Of course, I want to know!" And the test came up as POSITIVE! We were expecting our first child! Holy crap--talk about life changing! Life was about to change drastically and quickly, and for the better!

Alejandra Pregnant with Sebastian- Quitting Smoking

After we took the test we went to the doctor's and they also confirmed that we were indeed pregnant. We were both very excited and couldn't wait to tell people, but we figured we would

125

wait a few weeks. It was hard to contain the news. Like I said before, in my sobriety I learned to never get too high or never too low. We told very few people—just those that are close to us like our parents and our siblings, and then once we were further along we shared the news with everybody else. Honestly, the pregnancy was fun planning for our first child. Everything from creating the registry list for the baby shower, to patiently waiting for every Wednesday to come around when we would get the email on the weekly update of the size of my baby from Babycenter.com! It went from the size of a sesame seed, to a kumquat, to a lime, to a lemon; then to an orange, a cantaloupe, to a papaya, a butternut squash... It was cool seeing and monitoring the growth inside her belly and seeing the ultrasounds and all that good stuff.

Alejandra really hated smoking and the smell of smoke, and so did I. She could not understand why I couldn't quit. Neither she herself nor any of her family members ever smoked. It was a crutch that I just hadn't been ready to give up. I hate doing it and I felt ashamed. I hated the smell and spending money on it. I hated doing it, but I was addicted. I didn't smoke that much but I was addicted and couldn't quit on my own. With a newborn on the way one of the things I kept thinking about was that I didn't want the baby boy to be around the smoke and I certainly didn't want him to pick up the habit. Between deep down inside me wanting to quit and Alejandra hating it and now the fact that we were having a newborn--this was the final straw and another reason to stop.

"Stress will always be there; it is how you deal with it and perceive it."

126

This was the single most difficult habit to break. They say it is as addicting as heroin. I finally went back to the foundations for my sobriety. I was powerless over this addiction, just like I was with alcohol and other drugs. Just like with alcohol and drugs, my way of quitting wasn't working. In February 2012, I knew I had to do something. I needed help. So, I decided to try the nicotine lozenges. The suggested dosage was ridiculous, and I tried to adhere to the instructions from the beginning but felt that I didn't need to take that many of them, so I ended up taking them at different times that typically generated triggers. I was 100% ready to quit. I knew there would be stress at home, and work, and in life in general. It will be stressful with a newborn. Stress will always be there; it is how you deal with it and perceive it. Smoking has zero value and will not help with stress. It's just how you manage these stressful times and doing something stupid like smoking is not good for you it is not the answer how to manage those stressful situations. The lozenges worked! After a month or so I'd say probably 6 weeks, I stopped taking them. I found myself taking them less, and less and the cravings went away. What a freaking miracle. I was free.

On March 14th, 2012 our son Sebastian was born! At age 42 I'm now a dad! And now I instantly had a new hobby which was taking care of a newborn! I didn't enjoy the limited sleep at night and then trying to function at work as a Food Service Director; who would? I don't remember having too much energy after work and not sleeping that much but I could not wait to get home to see the little guy. Babies do not do much more than that, but I would simply just stare at him or let him sit in my lap while I was watching TV; that

127

was pretty cool. The weather in Boston was still cold but I enjoyed bundling him up and going for a walk with the stroller, which became my new hobby. I'm grateful that my father-in-law bought us a baby stroller. When we were looking at them and doing research, I knew that I wanted something that you can run with. I wasn't a runner but the little snap and go that we had with our other one was difficult to go over the hills, cracks, pebbles, sidewalks and broken streets of Cambridge, Belmont, and Waltham. I wanted something that was more durable and that could manage better than the other ones we had. I convinced Alejandra that I was planning on doing more walking, and that I do not want to have to keep stopping and lifting the damn thing up or getting tired stuck in cracks and shit. So, we got the "City Jogger" with the attachment that the snap and go Graco car seat could attach to the top of the stroller until his neck was strong enough. When his neck was strong enough, he could sit in the Baby Jogger. I had visions of jogging or running with him in it just because it's kind of fun--just like running with a shopping cart through the parking lot or flying on one of those things at IKEA from one side of the store to the other.

I could see myself jogging sometimes on the Minuteman Bike Path through the Paul Dudley Trail that goes along the river into Boston. I never envisioned running a marathon with a stroller to be honest with you but that happened. Not an official one, but that happened. So, for the next ten months I enjoyed watching him grow and taking him out for walks in pretty much any weather conditions unless it was really raining very hard or super cold. I would drop him off and pick him up at daycare 99% of the time in the stroller or sometimes even in the sled! A minimum day's mileage was two miles. It was a

128

half a mile to daycare and a half a mile back. We did that twice a day and then typically after work I picked him up from daycare and then we would leave and go two and a half miles to Harvard Square and then the two miles back home. I would pack the diaper bag, give him a few Cheerios and some milk and I would sit there at Peet's Coffee and have a pastry and a coffee. Me and my little guy spent a lot of time in Harvard Square! That was our favorite place to walk to. It started becoming pretty routine doing that three or four times a week. I looked forward to picking him up and going on an adventure together! A lot of friends complained that walking or running bothered their feet and knees. My feet didn't bother me and neither did my knees, and this became fairly easy. I didn't really keep track of the weekly miles I was doing yet but was probably averaging 5 miles a day during the week. On the weekends I probably averaged 10 total miles. If I had to guess, we probably logged 10,000 miles on it in five years!

Chapter 23

Arizona February 2013; Time Zone Change; Started More Distance Walking

Since moving from Arizona in 2009 we had not been back to visit. We still stayed in touch with the core group of friends. I feel like the time I lived in Arizona I was a little bit bored and I often said everything was like The Flintstones out here when Fred's driving. You see the same cactus, the same palm trees, the houses look the same, the same Circle K , the same Jack in the Box, the same Wendy's. Everything just kind of looks the same when you drive down the street. The desert is brown, the cacti are just kind of blah. Well, that's how it was perceived then. I know now the desert is beautiful in Arizona and it's what you make it and how you see it. It's what you *want* to see. I have spent time outdoors before but not nearly enough time in the mountain trails exploring. I think at the time in 2009 we were ready for a geographical change and fresh start as a couple and as individuals. Everything happens for a reason. That's the way it worked out and we made that decision to move. There's no way of figuring out what life would have been like if we stayed in Arizona, but I would just daydream thinking about it. We decided that we wanted to come out for a vacation during a long cold winter in Boston. Sebastian was 10.5 months old and had already flown once. We love to travel so we said let's do it, let's go to Arizona. We talked to our friends George and Sophie who had a child the same age as Sebastian and they invited us to stay with them in their new home. They live in Tempe, which was not too far away from where we lived before and they had space for us. The packing list was almost all about Sebastian. What are we

130

forgetting? I always like to bring items to be self-sufficient which includes coffee. Knowing where my coffee is and where the next one is coming from is comforting, as well as protein bars and snacks. I brought my Garmin GPS watch just in case!

We had a great flight out. Sebastian slept most of the way and the next thing we knew we were landing in Arizona, hell yeah! It was kind of surreal flying back to the state with so many different emotions. I started thinking about what we left behind here and started thinking about the hard times, but I started thinking about my sobriety too. It was now 3 years into my sobriety. I was a different person. How would people perceive me and how would I perceive them? I perceived everybody else just the same—it was just that I had a different outlook on life.

We arrived at George and Sophie's. It was so good to see them and then meet their son Kosta. The two kids are basically 10 and 9 months-old and all they did was crawl, make noises and eat snacks together, but it was cool to kind of see them interact. It was cool to see our friends having a baby too. I started thinking about what it would be like to live in Arizona again and watch the kids grow together. The first day was fine but the night wasn't great. We were grateful to be in someone else's house and not have to pay for a hotel room. We were grateful for the hospitality and the wonderful food that Sophie made. However, it was a two-hour time zone difference from Boston to Arizona and Sebastian woke up at 3:00 AM Arizona time--which would have been 5:00 AM Boston time like he usually did. He was a really good baby but just like any baby they tell you when they want something. They tell you when they want milk by crying because they can't talk, or they tell you when they poop in their diaper and need a diaper change, or they cry because they can't talk. 3:00 in the morning we gave him a bottle of milk and changed his diaper, and he was WIDE AWAKE. I remember sitting up in the bedroom we were in, all three of us. I'm thinking, now what? What do we do, give another bottle of milk? Sebastian was a great sleeper and quite often when I put him in the stroller and gave him some milk, he would fall asleep.

After half an hour or 45 minutes I got up and said I'll be right back. I went ahead, prepared my iced coffee, grabbed my bar, two bottles of milk and packed up the diaper bag with 3 diapers and wipes, some snacks and a change of clothes and told Alejandra I was going for a walk. She said, "It's 3:45 in the morning; where are you going?" I told her they live in a cul-de-sac and I was just going to do some circles until he fell asleep and then I'll come back in. Well, I got bored pretty soon after doing three-quarters of a little loop and I found my way walking around the neighborhood. I quickly became bored with the neighborhood, so I went out to the main road. Maybe some white noise of some cars going by--the few that were out at the time would put him to sleep. I did notice that he was kicking his feet doing gurgling, and just enjoying himself making noises, blowing bubbles and so I just kept going. And then I found myself going underneath the I-60 and thought to myself, oh wow I remember we used to go to South Mountain somewhere kind of close to here! I could just kind of walk to the top of the foothills and take pictures; maybe I'll head that way. I had the GPS watch that my mother had given me a and I was already somewhere around a mile and a half. I was kind of impressed because I wasn't really paying attention to how far I was going. I had my iced coffee and my bar in my belly, so I was up. once I'm up I'm up and have coffee in me I'm usually pretty good to go.

All of a sudden, I said yeah, I'm going to South Mountain and that's exactly what I did. I went to and through the town of Guadalupe, which is not necessarily that safe but there was really nobody out at that time. Then we crossed the bridge over the I-10 and then zigzagged through a subdivision because I didn't know about the entrance at Pima Canyon and entered the desert. It was still pitch-black and of course I didn't have a flashlight. I just had my Blackberry flip phone which didn't give us too much light. I remember being greeted by two large saguaros, one of the left one on the right and I can't even really see anything past that. It was such a cool feeling. Every step I took I started thinking, I wonder what's out there. I have the stroller and Sebastian's kind of bouncing around but he's loving it. He's just looking around, still making noise, kicking his feet and waving his hands. So, I cautiously kept going. We found our way to where the bathrooms are at Pima Canyon parking lot. I could see the mountains and the foothills. I decided to go up one of those foothills and I could start to see the horizon towards Mesa and Four Peaks skyline, as it started to get a little bit brighter. So, I said let's go to the top and take some pictures of the sunrise. A lot of the time I needed to carry the stroller because it wouldn't go over the rugged terrain there. I probably spilled a little bit of iced coffee and stumbled a few times but then we went onward and upward. We stood up there and waited for the sunrise for about a half an hour. It was spectacular, as I think I took over 200 pictures and posted them to

133

Facebook immediately. I wasn't digging Facebook back then, but I couldn't wait to share these pictures and really show the enthusiasm and the feeling that I had at that time. The feeling was a burning fire inside of me. A seed was planted.

We had logged somewhere around five miles already and saw the sunrise. I knew that we had at least five miles to go back. This was pretty crazy as I was the only one out there, and who would believe me? Well, if it's posted on Facebook it happened, right? I felt alive when I was walking, I thoroughly enjoyed it and if Sebastian could speak at the time, I am 100% sure he would have said the same! I FELT ALIVE! I HAD FILLED THE VOID! I was proud that I had gone that far. I knew I could do it. This changed me into a distance walker and laid the groundwork for me to become a distance runner. I hadn't felt that fire in years! Now I had something to look forward to. I felt almost like an athlete. and I would be going farther than I had ever gone before on the roads, on the trails of a mountain, and then back. I couldn't believe the beauty of everything around me. I just wanted to go back. As we started down after I took all those pictures of the sunrise, I heard some weird dogs howling. Those are coyotes! Oftentimes when you hear the coyotes, they are much farther away then they seem to be. I could see there were probably twenty of them, which is crazy because I don't think I've ever seen that many coyotes at once in all my time here. The photos of them didn't really come out that well because my Blackberry isn't that advanced, but I tried. This was one of the coolest days of my life. It changed me. I don't remember which way we went, which trails or what else we did but we did tack on

134

another two or three miles there, and then went back and ended up getting around 12 miles total.

I remember getting back around eight 8:30AM, opening up the door and discovering that nobody was awake yet. We came in and woke up Alejandra and couldn't wait to tell her where I went! She was like, "Nooooooooooooooooo you did not! No, you did not go that far; no you did not go through Guadeloupe; no you did not go to South Mountain and no, you didn't risk my child's life near a pack of coyotes looming over everything   else just mentioned above." The odds of coyotes attacking are not that great, so I wasn't worried about Sebastian's safety. I told her to look at Facebook or hear my phone; look at all these pictures, WTF! I told her this was one of the greatest days in my life and then I was a new person and Sebastian really, really enjoyed it. She said, "My God next time I don't want you going to Guadalupe; it's not safe, especially in the dark! If you're going to do something like that, take the car and park, and go from there." My legs were pretty tired and so was my whole body from having to carry the stroller so many times over the rocks and bumps. I don't think we did too much that day except for eating and recovering! I remember plotting my next journey which ended up being more miles the next day in South Mountain, but I drove there. I don't remember how many miles I did, but probably six or seven on the trails there and I think I actually went up and down the east loop. I can't confirm that, but what I can confirm is that I felt really alive again and I loved every minute of it so did Sebastian. We left at like 5:00 AM this time and still got home before anybody woke up!

135

Sebastian and I had a new routine on vacation! We started each day off with a hike or a walk exploring. The next day we stayed on the roads. I had worked at ASU on the main campus prior to leaving for the Beijing Olympic project. This is one of the largest campuses in the United States and I remember working catering there for a few months. We did a lot of walking because there were so many students and it was hard to drive. It was almost easier just to walk. At the time I hated it, as it was hot out. But now I had a different perspective, and I went up and down each street, cut through the sidewalks to different yards and walked to all the different parts of the campus with the stroller. We did somewhere around 12 miles just on the ASU Campus which was pretty cool. All before anyone woke up, including the students. All of a sudden, I realized—holy shit, I am a distance walker. Three days in a row I had somewhere around 30 miles logged walking. That's pretty crazy. I think I took a day off because my feet were killing me. My back was killing me, even my neck and shoulders from them being elevated from pushing the stroller. A day of rest was earned and deserved. But what do I do in my free time in the morning when Sebastian wakes up? Being in motion like that was overstimulating and it caught up to him because he was super tired that day. I went for another distance walk the following day and then it was time to go home.

"This trip back to Arizona shaped me into the person I am today"
This little trip back to Arizona changed me and shaped me into the person I am today. I think I caught the endurance bug again! I started thinking on the plane what if I ran? I could go further, and I could get there faster, what a crazy concept! DUH! *Just imagine; I could go places farther away if I ran.* This concept resurfaced down the road. I couldn't wait to get home and start plotting and planning

136

routes that would take me farther than I had ever gone before back in Massachusetts.

Chapter 24
Instead of Climbing the Walls, I spent Time on Google® Maps

If I could run, I could go farther, and get there faster. I kept thinking about this. Every now and then I would try to run but I would be completely winded and have side stitches and shin splints. Running sucks. I have wondered for years why anybody would want to run--especially in the rain and the snow or in the cold. I used to look at them as they were sick, like addicts, they cannot help themselves. Are they sick, do they have to run? Like literally, what's wrong with these people? Why do they have to run in the rain? Why do they have to run and why can't they just run the next day or wait till it stops running, stupid morons! I felt they were addicted to running. "Oh I need to run 10 miles today so I'm going to go out and run." But wow, that's commitment! They might have been addicted, but who was I to judge them? At least they're doing something positive, at least they are not abusing alcohol or drugs. I had no idea "how to run." What I didn't know at the time was how to pace myself. When I tried to run, I would run pretty much at a 5K pace right from the get-go and of course I would be winded. That's not how you run and certainly not how you start. You should do some sort of warm up or start your run slower. Otherwise, you will be gassed, and you will have shin splints and you will be hating life and you probably will never enjoy the sport of running. I learned the right way to run from my friend Randy, who trained with me. You should be able to run and to hold a conversation. If not, you're running too fast and will experience shortness of breath; your shins will hurt, and you'll get those painful side splits.

I grew up spectating the Boston Marathon. I think from the age of five until the age of thirty-four I might have missed two marathons in person. They say you have to picture yourself doing something and I could picture myself running the marathon someday. Even at a young age I thought how cool that would be. I also dreamed of being a baseball player and other things. I can honestly say that I was just dreaming at a young age and that was not a goal. Sometimes we would see the elites pass by and then go home. Sometimes we would get there later and see the charity runners, and the middle of the pack runners. If you watch it in Newton near Heartbreak Hill, or any of the hills for that matter, that's the point in the race where you see a lot of courage and also see a lot of people really struggle. People collapse. People cramping up. It is a very popular place for people to watch The Boston Marathon so there's a lot of emotional people. This is a great place for people to see their loved ones in the crowd and vice-versa, the loved ones would see them. It's always such a cool vibe about this day, Patriots Day in Boston. I never had to work on that day and if I did, I would take the day off because it was special to me. When I was a teenager, we go to the Red Sox games and get tickets the morning of the game for the 11:00 AM traditional game at Fenway Park. When the game got out around 1:30pm, the city would shut down and you could not even take the green line back. You had no place to go so we would go to Kenmore Square, which is right near Fenway and stay there and watch the marathon for a couple of hours.

Once I started my drinking career, we would start drinking on this day pretty early--like 8AM early. Several years in a row I would rollerblade into Boston and a couple of years I also rode my bike in. There were always parties, whether at Northeastern, BU, BC, or just in apartments or frat houses in the city. We would go to bars and the parties, then go to more bars with the parties all day then have to go all the way home. These were some of the best parties. I thought it was pretty amazing to be able to drink like a fish from early in the morning until the afternoon and then somehow find a way to rollerblade or bike all the way to my house for more than eight miles. I knew how far it was. It's just hard to comprehend when you're on foot, on rollerblades, or on a bike. My whole day was a marathon. There would be carnage, and statements like this on the way home, "This sucks. I am never going to make it, this is taking forever, I just want to be done with this!" I knew that I had to pace myself because I still had to get home in one piece.

Rollerblading and bike riding in the city Boston on Patriots Day Marathon Monday became an annual thing. I took different friends in there and it was always an adventure. It became one of my favorite days. It was pretty cool drinking all day and adventuring around different points of the city watching the marathon and finding our way home all fucked up. I mean it wasn't easy obviously, even rollerblading twenty plus miles was not easy, sober!. And just like in a marathon, you need nutrition to keep going. You will hear voices in your head that can make you stop if

139

you listen to them. You know—the negative chatter that says, "You can't make it, you're starting to slow down, you're tired, you're in pain, you should stop. Maybe this is not for you." This was a challenge each year that I embraced. After all, I practiced doing this--just that this particular day we tended to drink a lot more. The house parties were typically keg parties and we would do keg stands, funnels and drinking games. My nutrition was a lot different back then. We found ourselves surviving off low budget food such as McDonald's, slices of pizza from somewhere, and we would splurge on a sausage, pepper, and onion from The Sausage King. This was the typical nutrition of our endurance event. On the way home I would think about the different runners that we saw falling down and cramping up and I wondered what it would be like to run the actual Marathon. I smoked weed and cigarettes and even though I was active, I could not even think about running for more than one hundred yards. At that time, actually running for more than two minutes would be impossible. I would be winded and rightfully so. In my 20's I dreamed about doing the marathon, but this was far-fetched, as I was in no condition to do it. I didn't even run yet.

Chapter 25
2012 Boston Marathon

In 2012 Alejandra wanted to go to the marathon, so we took the green line into Kenmore early. We walked around to take pictures in the city, and then found a nice spot at the finish line near Marathon Sports on Boylston Street. We stayed there for about an hour and I think we popped and out of a few of the stores there just to check stuff out. For the most part we had a sweet spot on the sidewalk to see the elite runners finish. On the other side of the street there were a bunch of vendors passing out food items, water, gummies and all that good stuff. After staring at the different logos for a while and smelling all the smells I insisted on going across the street. We stocked up on some food and kind of walked towards Fenway away from the finish line and the crowds started to form. We made it past a corner that was pretty congested on Hereford. Go figure; they were doing a little bit of construction on the sidewalk, so we really had to squeeze by. I remember there were people with bikes, backpacks, baby strollers, which was super annoying because you couldn't pass by and you got hit in the shin with a pedal or in the face with a backpack or in the back of a calf with a tire. That got old pretty quick, and it was annoying just trying to pass by. It was like trying to get to the front row of a punk rock concert. You are literally having to push your way through the crowds of people who are getting annoyed as well. This was a huge mistake.

It started getting late, meaning the elites were probably going to arrive pretty soon, because the marathon started an hour and 45 minutes ago, so we decided to try to make our way back past that

142

corner. It wasn't happening, no way no how. We had lost our spot at the finish line that we had staked out in the beginning. Alejandra kept telling me we should have stayed, we should have stayed, you should have stayed at the finish line! In retrospect we should have planned better, and I should have brought snacks, but I didn't. What can we do now? I told her that one of the best places to watch the marathon was Fenway which was a mile away. That's what we did; we made our way that way. There's a part of the course that goes under the road and is now a Boston Strong Banner over there. Anyway, we're right about there and then we saw and heard motorcycle sirens and the cheers of the crowd started to roar which meant one thing. The elites were coming through. We stopped there and I was on my tippy toes. I'm 6 '2" but I could barely see and snap a few pictures on my phone. Alejandra is much shorter and couldn't see anything; she was pissed at me, rightfully so. To this day she never has let me live it down. We moved to a spot up on the hill a little further down towards Kenmore Square and watched the rest of the elites come through and then stayed and watched for another hour or so. We walked to Fenway and hung out in the crowds there. As the game got it brought back flashbacks of being all messed up right in the middle of it having to pee. I started thinking about all the madness that would happen on this day and what a miracle it was to be there with Alejandra in the city and being sober. We were standing in the city at the 25-mile mark at the historic Boston Marathon with my wife. Life had changed and changed for the better. Sebastian was a little over a month and home with my parents. I thought about him, how lucky I was and thought about bringing him there with us in the future and thought about how cool it would be if he and Alejandra could watch me run one

143

year. That was just a pipe-dream. Back then I thought you had to be a special kind of athlete to even run the marathon. Later I thought you can do anything if you put a plan together. If I could quit smoking and drinking that would give me the confidence to do it.

April, 2013

"I had the fever, the fire and the desire to run"

I remember reading an article about local runners that were running the Boston Marathon, the reasons why they train and the causes that they ran for. One of them was about a friend "Randy" from high school. I wouldn't say he was a friend in high school, but he was a classmate, and he was running for the Melanoma Foundation of New England. His first wife died from melanoma cancer and he was running for their foundation to raise funds for a cure and to raise awareness about skin cancer and protecting yourself from the sun. It was a very touching story. He did not seem like the runner type to me. In my mind he didn't fit with the prototypical runner. He was an HVAC guy, blue collar, and not what I envision a runner to be. I thought that was pretty cool that he was doing this Marathon, which was a life goal of his, and in memory of his wife. He was turning the tragedy of losing his wife into something good in hopes of helping others. I remember visiting Alejandra at work and bringing Sebastian in the stroller. I tried to run on the Minuteman bike path behind her work in Lexington. I remember we went for a walk and I said, "I'm going to run from here to there, from this tree to that tree." It was probably about a hundred yards. And the same thing happened as before; I ran too fast, I was winded and had that

144

pain in my gut called stitches and I was completely out of breath. My throat hurt. I had the fever, the fire, and the desire to run. I started thinking about how cool it would be to actually train properly and run the historic Boston Marathon. I knew there were other marathons, and I knew about the world marathons. I just didn't know how many marathons there were everywhere. As far as races, I knew about 5K's and half marathons and full marathons but that's it. I knew that the Boston Marathon was the Super Bowl of all marathons. I knew it was the oldest running marathon and I knew that was the one that everybody wanted to run. I started thinking, well maybe if I train, I could actually run it next year. Which is crazy because I can't even run one hundred yards. I always believe you gotta start somewhere. I just have to start with the desire, I guess. The first step is wanting to do something, the next step is commitment.

I think I probably Googled registration for the Boston Marathon and was kind of confused because you had to qualify or run for a charity? It said the registration was closed so I said I have time to investigate, and I'll just register when the registration becomes open, if that's what I want to do. That was my thought process. I remember running from side street to side street sometimes and I would pick up Sebastian from daycare. So, it was run for 15 seconds, stop, carefully cross the road and then run 15 seconds, repeat until I got home. Sometimes I would hear a tune on the headphones and just be inspired and run for a stretch going into Harvard Square until I was winded.

Chapter 26

2013 Boston Marathon

The 2013 Marathon was approaching, and we started talking about spectating this year. I wanted to bring Sebastian to the marathon but not near the finish line. I remember how many people and with the other strollers, bikes and backpacks he would not be able to see anything. He was too young anyway so it would have been selfish to bring them there and more of a pain in the ass. Alejandra thought it would be better if we went to the hills of Newton to watch from there. We went to Heartbreak Hill and had him in the stroller; then he wanted out so I carried him for a little bit and I even put him in the front pouch thing--whatever those are called and let him watch and kind of bounce around, kick his feet and wave his hands. We got there in the afternoon after the elites had already passed by and we saw the charity runners and others that were on pace to finish in four to four and half hours. We saw a lot of runners at their breaking points. Hello lovely hills of Newton. We watched soldiers march with flags and 40-pound rucksacks. We watched wheelchairs and people with prosthetic limbs running, and really hardcore runners with great determination to finish. This was super inspiring for me when I started thinking if they can do it I can. You have to believe in yourself; you have to believe you can do something. You have to envision what it would look like finishing. Like I said before, the first thing you need to have is desire, the second is commitment. I started thinking about committing to running.

After spending a couple of hours there I figured it'd be best if we went home. Sebastian was still only a year old and we were tired

146

too. We still had a few things we wanted to do that day, so we went home, regrouped and then I insisted that we walk to Target, which was exactly a mile away from our apartment. I hate the mall to begin with a little bit and it gets a little crazy in there, so I remember just kind of walking around with Sebastian in the stroller while Alejandra was at Things Remembered. I kept kind of circling around and checking on her to see when she was going to be done. I noticed a few people stopping and pointing and staring inside the Marcou Jewelers at the TV. I don't like to be nosy, but they all had this strange look of concern. So, I pushed the stroller towards the store, stopped to catch a glimpse and saw the closed captioning on the screen reading, "Possible Marathon Bombings, Suspects on the Loose." What! I tiptoed up towards the TV; nobody said a word and we collectively just watched with our jaws basically on the ground in disbelief. We could have been at that finish line. We thought about going to the finish line anyway and probably would have. If I didn't listen to my wife, that's where we would be. I stayed there and watched the TV for a few minutes just so I could get the facts straight. Then I walked over, told Alejandra and she couldn't believe it. I showed her on the TV; it was really eerie and obviously tragic and surreal. How could somebody put bombs at the finish line of the Boston Marathon? What type of people would do this? Terrorists. They didn't know who or what at the time and they were piecing things together by the minute, but the Boston Marathon was stopped, and runners were rerouted off the course. What? In our city?

I remember looking down at my phone, which earlier had 60% battery power. When I opened it up, the notifications started

147

blowing up my phone as I started reading them. People from our family in Mexico, people from Arizona, and just friends in general. Family was checking on us because they knew we were going to be at the Marathon, we had posted pictures earlier and they were hoping that we were okay. The notifications completely drained the battery on my phone. We went home, plugged in our phones to recharge them and we put on the news. We were glued to the TV as new information started rolling in. We responded to messages and sent messages to the people we know to let them know we were okay. People kept asking us what happened. I started thinking about all the runners and spectators that could have possibly been hurt from the explosions. What type of pure evil would do this to our city? Indeed, it was terrorists that were the suspects but local terrorists? Whoever it was, all we can do is pray that they got caught and pray that the injuries were minimal. We came to find out the two brothers that were the suspects in hiding were living within a 2-mile radius of our apartment! This was unbelievable. The authorities had information on who they were, where they lived, stores they would shop at, and places they would hang out--which are all in our neck of the woods. The bombs were made out of pressure cookers which were purchased at Target, the same one we were at the previous day. That's crazy. These terrorists lived among us. The odds are pretty good that we crossed paths with them at least once. Especially Sebastian and I, as these were the streets that we walked quite often.

The night of the high-speed chase when one of the brothers was killed, we were already in bed. I remember the next morning taking our dog Luci out to go to the bathroom and I saw one of our neighbors, "drunk dude Dave." He asked me what I was doing outside. I said what? What do you mean, what am I doing outside? He said you didn't hear? You're not supposed to be outside? I said, whatever Dave. This guy wasn't too credible. He was a maintenance guy for a building for a little bit and he drank quite a bit. He definitely had an issue with alcohol. Whether you were fucked up or not he was pretty serious and sure about what he said. He said, "The terrorists are on the loose--or at least one of them was. There was a chase, and they don't know where one of them is, and they want us to stay indoors. It's all over the news. We're supposed to be in lock-down; if you don't believe me go turn on any of the news cameras news channels." So I was like, okay? I had no reason not to believe him, who would make something like this up? I thanked him and then went inside and put the TV on. The first thing I saw was SWAT teams on top of the roof of one of the breakfast diners that we went to the day before which was the morning of the marathon! WOW. They kept showing different camera angles. There were snipers in different areas of streets and on the rooftops right where I usually walk every day. Apparently overnight one of the suspects fled after the high-speed chase and was hiding in the perimeter, which was a half a mile from my house. Holy shit. I woke up Alejandra and told her. I sent the people on our second and third floor a message as well. I called my mom. This was crazy; you weren't supposed to go outside. He could be hiding in the bushes, under a car, in a tree or could have broken into my apartment--who the hell knows. I started thinking what can we do as a city and as a state to make a statement? I can pick up a shovel. I could grab a knife and protect my family. I get that but what could I do to show

149

them--whoever they are (the terrorists) that we're not afraid. That you can't fuck with us. You're are fucking with the wrong City.

To quote David Ortiz: "This is our fucking City."

I started thinking about running a little bit more. I seriously started thinking about running the 2014 Boston Marathon. We cannot live in fear and one way to show that we're not afraid is to rebuild and come together. There is strength in numbers; we can become stronger. If we show that we're not afraid in unity we won't let them win. I could become a runner and I could run this Boston Marathon and run in unity with 32,000 of my closest friends. What is stopping me? I had 360 days to train and get ready for it. Why couldn't I? I started running a little bit here and there but more or less the same, from one street to the other with Sebastian in the stroller. I enjoyed it as I was getting to where I wanted to go a little faster. I could go a little bit farther each time with a walk run ratio. I still did not consider myself a runner or that I was actually going for a run. I walked more than I ran, but I ran in spurts.

Chapter 27

The Real Birth of My Running Career-Early May, 2013

We had some good friends, Enrique and Maritza that we used to hang out with a lot when we lived in Arizona together and Enrique had accepted a position to work at Corning Glass in Corning, New York. Corning is located in Western New York and has long cold winters just like Boston. I didn't think they would survive one year there but they actually thrived. Maritza got a job at Corning as well and they settled in nicely there. I know that they did not embrace the cold but they certainly coexisted. Enrique finally was able to quit smoking. I remember seeing on Facebook that he ran the Disney Half Marathon and The Wineglass Half Marathon, and I was super impressed. At the time I didn't even know how far a half marathon was. The fact that he was able to quit smoking and decided to become a runner was great. He was pretty much living a sedentary lifestyle and overweight when we lived in Arizona. It was awesome to follow his fitness and running journey on Facebook. Seeing him change and drop all this weight was very inspiring to me. If he could change and run why couldn't I? They had invited us out for the Memorial Day weekend and mentioned there was an annual event called Glassfest in downtown Corning. There would be street vendors and crafts, as well as all different types of food. There was going to be a puppet show, and also Amazing Magic Joe, musical acts and other things planned for the long weekend. I noticed that there was a Glassfest 8K road race. No idea how long an 8k was and all I did was ask Enrique if he was going to run. He said something along the lines of, "I'll run if you do!" My reply was, "Sign me up!" I know myself and I know that I need to be

151

accountable. Especially for my recovery. If I say I'm going to do something, or I say I'm going to be there, I'm going to be there and I'm going to do it. I committed to him and committed to myself. I told Alejandra and she was kind of surprised! I had an anxious feeling more like butterflies inside of me, and my heart was racing a little bit once I committed. I ran three times prior to the 8K with Sebastian: four miles, three miles, and two and a half miles. I ran most of those miles as if I was on a mission! Hay was in the barn!

Glassfest 8k Corning, NY: 5-25-2013

I don't want to say I was ready because I didn't know what I was in for, but I wasn't going to be any more ready than I was right then and there at the starting line. That's true today for any distance whether it's a 5k, or a hundred miler. You put the time in and you show up. There's no more time for training, no more time for anything. In truth, I trained very little for this race. Sebastian was all bundled up and ready in the stroller. It was a balmy 45 degrees with 40-mile per hour headwinds and I'm pushing this kid in a stroller, really? Maybe the starting line was not the best place to ask how far 8k was, but I asked! I had a general idea, but I wasn't sure. An 8k is almost 5 miles; crap salad-- I haven't run distance, what am I doing here? I 'm in a corral with a bunch of other people and this guy's talking over a PA system and they're about to sing the national anthem and I'm stuck in this crowd with No Way Out. I committed to this. I said I wanted to run. It felt great to have something to train for and here we were.

"I was so proud of myself because I wanted to quit but I didn't quit."

152

Ready for the gun to go off. They sang the National Anthem and then it was 10, 9, 8, 7, 6, 5, 4 ,3 2, 1 and we are off! I was all bundled up in a Bruins shirt and had two layers on the top and two on the bottom. Sebastian was in like a pink sleep sack; he had a bottle of milk and we were running. It was not expected to be this cold or windy! I was running faster than I ever ran before as I was caught up in a pack of other runners. When you're in a race, especially shorter distances, you're typically faster. You're caught up in the moment and you have adrenaline plus you are running with other people. I started off a little bit too strong. I started getting tired, winded and discouraged. After a mile or so I was tired of getting beaten down by the wind, and every time another runner would pass me I would get pissed and felt demoralized. I had thoughts of tripping them up but all I did was curse to myself in my head. I hated everything about this. I wanted to quit so badly! I couldn't wait for it to be over and I was super disappointed. I was super disappointed because I thought I finally found something that I liked. My dreams of running Boston were shattered, and I guess I probably had false hope about this new hobby of running. My body and my mind took a beating. I realized that I was at the halfway point and that was the pinnacle of the race. Why quit now? Why turn around now? I made it this far. I can get to the end! I still had doubts because the wind was just thrashing me around, pushing the stroller and made it pretty much impossible to push through sometimes. We went over this bridge and I did not think I was going to make it. I had not much left in my tank, my legs were smoked, and the wind was pushing me back, literally. I made it over that bridge and when I got to the other side, I could see crowds of people. And there was Alejandra and Maritza with her kids all

153

bundled up. I was about to pass them and then head towards the track and I could see the inflatable finish line. That put a huge smile on my face and adrenaline started to carry me towards them. Then I was on my last legs and taking my last breaths and I was about to finish…and I finished! It was one of the greatest feelings in my life and one of my greatest accomplishments. It was only an 8K but this was just the start of something bigger. I was so proud of myself because I did not quit. I wanted to quit but I didn't quit. I committed to this. It sucked. I hated every moment of it but I finished. What an emotional rollercoaster. I was really proud of myself.

When I crossed the finish line, I stopped my watch and was greeted by a volunteer that had a glass Medallion, a medal for me? I didn't realize we were getting medals, wow this thing was solid! I felt like I just won a gold medal or finished in first place. My official time was 46 minutes and 17 seconds finishing in 309th place out of 549 runners--not bad! All things considered, I did really well. Especially since this was really like my fourth time running. I was really happy with my time, but I knew I could shave at least a few minutes off here and there. I knew that once I started running more and got stronger, I would be able to do a lot less walking. I knew that if I didn't run with the stroller, I would be faster. I knew that if there weren't 40 mile an hour winds, I would be faster. I knew that I had to train more; I know that hard work pays off. Enrique finished about 5 minutes ahead of me. We all met somewhere on the field and celebrated, exchanging some congratulations, hugs and fist bumps. I enjoyed the camaraderie of the running community. I remember just looking around soaking it all up, savoring the moment. Besides the glass medallion I remember getting water, a banana and some gummies. I was shaky at best and pretty depleted as I had never run this hard before. I remember being on cloud nine still as I still had that "runner's high."

When we arrived back at our friends' home, I asked Enrique if I could use his computer. We stayed with them before so I would ask to use his computer so I could just check email or check ESPN or to check scores for my fantasy sports team roster. "Yes, what for?" I said I want to see if there were any races or anything like that near Belmont or Waltham where we lived in Massachusetts. I remember seeing some sort of Santa Claus run in Harvard Square, a couple of the races there and remember seeing some cones in the road and runners with numbers on their shorts and shirts running through Waltham and Watertown before. I Googled something like road running races Waltham Massachusetts. The first thing that came up was the RAW Series (Race Around Waltham). I came to find out there was a 5k the following weekend on the 1st of June. It was the Saint Jude's 5K. I asked Alejandra if I could register. She said, "Are you sure you want to do that?" I said, "Yeah, if I ran an 8k, I can run a 5k! And plus it's in Waltham at St.Jude's School. I can definitely do it. I'll run with Sebastian."

Chapter 28
RAW SERIES 6-1-2013

I usually show up two or three hours ahead of time because I hate being late and really like to soak up the scene. I was one of the first in line to get my bib and pinned it on my shorts. The sun was coming up and I already started to feel pretty hot. I remember drinking lots of water and having to pee like fifteen times, which could have been a combination of the bundle of nerves, or the water, or the gallon of coffee I drank first thing in the morning. Regardless, I went back and forth inside the school to go to the bathroom. I saw a couple of people I recognized, chatted it up with them and met some new friends. I could really sense that a lot of people knew each other, and this was a community. I didn't feel like a loner, but I felt like a newbie. Here we go again. It's time to line up for the start of the race. On your marks, get set, go! It was really hot, and I had never run in the heat before. This is a flat course and watching speed demons spend time pass me was humbling. I said a few serenity prayers. I could only control what I was doing; their fitness and their outcome was out of my control. I had no idea who most of them were, or if they had been running for years. I basically started to tell myself to shut up, push this stroller and run! I still had that same feeling every time someone passed me-- a little bit discouraging but I kept reminding myself I've never run much before and to be easy on myself. We are learning in recovery not to beat ourselves up. Just like the other race and in some of my other training runs.

I started off a little too strong so at the one-mile marker I had to lay off the gas a bit. It was so cool to be running in the neighborhood area that I went to elementary school in. I passed by some friends' homes I grew up with and passed by a Dunkin Donuts I went to often and our Petco, and then started down a road I drove down a zillion times-- then over the tracks back to Warrendale where I went to elementary school and on to the finish line at St Jude's. I finished with a time of 26 minutes and 6 seconds--good enough for 57th place out of 247 runners and mind you I was pushing Sebastian. This race felt hard but not as hard as the first one. It was a little bit shorter distance, a little bit flatter and no wind. I was really, really hot. I remember drinking like two or three waters and dumping one on my head; then I ate popsicles and hot dogs. How cool is this? Hot dogs for breakfast? I thought I only did that when I drank heavily! Not that many people were eating the hot dogs, so they were pushing them on people. I think I had six or seven--nothing in moderation. I left there with a tummy ache but the runner's high overrode that. I couldn't wait to do another race; perhaps I was hooked on racing.

RAW SERIES- Summer of 2013

RAW is an acronym for Race Around Waltham. The RAW Series was created by Tim and Kathy Irving in 2012. They did it to promote a healthy lifestyle and encourage people to start running in Waltham. The Irving's started with a half- dozen races, mostly at a 5K distance. There was a 4 miler called the Tailgate Trot. 4 miles is not much farther than the 3.1 miles of a 5k but the course had four tough miles. I knew the course. Basically, you ran from The Wave Sports Pub, which was the sports bar that I used to get into lot of trouble, and then you ran up the hill out of the parking lot, down the main road across the Waverley Oaks Rd, the main road from where I grew up, then took a right on Beaver Street past Bentley College, up a hill and around a steep corner. You went up a relentless hill until it leveled off at the two-mile mark and then it was slightly down and then you turned right on Trapelo Road and it was down and then right on Waverley Oaks, back into the parking lot and finished at The Wave. Not your typical race, little bit more difficult than the St. Jude's for sure. Especially pushing someone in the stroller! I registered online and I was up for this challenge too.

"I was hooked on racing and borderline addicted to racing"

I was hooked on racing and borderline addicted to racing. I couldn't wait for this race. It's kind of all I thought about during the week. I got a couple light runs in because it was a week after the St. Jude's 5K. I used to get pretty sore from running that hard because I was not used to the pounding. My training runs were easier, and I was still getting used to actually how to run. So, I thought I had to run on Tuesday and Thursday in preparation for Saturday's big 4 miler.

6-7-13 Tailgate Trot

I walked down to the parking lot with Sebastian in the stroller and there was a light sprinkle, just enough to get you wet so he was all bundled up and so was I. I could see where the race was and started to walk towards it and all of a sudden, a silver pickup truck with loud exhaust comes bombing down the hill and stops next to me and says, " Holy shit ,Henry Ward! "Figures you have a Bruins

159

shirt on!" I'm a pretty big hockey fan but I had no idea what to wear for this event--plus it was cold and rainy, what the hell do runners wear when it's cold and rainy anyways? Raincoats will overheat you, no? I'd see people running in light jackets or just in tank tops. I hate being cold and I hate being wet, so I bundled up. The rain jacket I bought just in case was too stuffy, so I threw it aside in the stroller and just had my Bruin's shirt on with a base layer underneath. It was Randy from high school! "Hey man, what's up Randy!" He said, "What are you doing guy?" " I am gonna run in this tailgate trot thing." He said, "Oh yeah I am too". "Cool, I'll see you over there."

I met him over there and we chatted it up. It had been 24 years since I had seen him. I mentioned to him that I saw the article in the newspaper about the Marathon he was running, and he told me they got rerouted two miles from the finish line and didn't finish. His brother Tommy was running with him, too. Tommy also came down to run the Tailgate Trot. I was in awe that I was going to be running this race with two people that ran the Boston Marathon. I looked at them like elite runners or celebrities. Someone told me early in my running career that running with people that are faster than you can make you a stronger runner. I looked around in the starting corral and realized I saw a lot of people that I recognized from the St. Jude's race, but I also saw a lot of people that I knew from high school, as well as people from Waltham in general. Some people I knew personally, some people I just recognized. But I mean at least I felt like part of the community. Runners are cool people; everybody was cool there.

160

Prior to the start I remember the routine was peeing fifteen times, chatting it up with people to ease the nerves, the butterflies and then it was time to run. I felt fine until we started going up the hill. That damn hill stopped me in my tracks, and I hit a wall, just like the bridge did in Corning, NY. Several people passed us going and as we had to walk the hill. And then I kind of grinded it out until we got to the halfway point and drank some water. After turning the corner onto Trapelo road heading to the 3-mile mark it was time for the home stretch. I passed a bunch of people that I went to high school with. It wasn't about, "Yeah, I passed you, I beat you--anything like that", but it was a good gauge for me mentally and physically to see where I was at. There were a few runners a couple of yards ahead of me. I tried to stay with them and use them as pacers, hang with them as long as I could and it kind of pushed me to go a little bit faster. I started using that mentality to kind of ride with a pack, find people that are right around my pace or a little bit faster, and hang with them as long as I could. I ran the last two miles balls to the wall and even though I was winded I just found the strength to push myself to my limits to finish strong. I realized you can run on a lot harder than you think you can, and a lot of this is in the head. You have to put the time in but sometimes when the going gets tough, mentally tough can push you through and you do well. I was like fuck this let's get this done. Sometimes I would think that the faster I finish, the faster I do not have to do this anymore! It sucks breathing very heavily; I'm not sure anyone likes it! On the other hand, this is crazy because I enjoy doing it, right? I finished this race in 35 minutes and 48 seconds--good enough for 67th Place. I was pretty happy with my effort and couldn't wait for the next race.

161

I looked at the calendar and the next race was not until September. What am I going to do all summer? I was talking to Randy after the race and he said there are some websites you can go to that have 5ks half-marathons, 10ks whatever the distance you might want. "Check out www.coolrunning.com." He gave me a couple other websites and his phone number and said we should go for a run sometime. So, I took him up on that offer. We started running together when we had time.

Chapter 29

Changing one Addiction for Another- Addicted to 5k Races

"Running changed my outlook, my attitude; I was more motivated"

After finding this cool running website it quickly became my favorite thing on the internet. I started scouring this page to see which 5Ks I could run. I found a Tory row 5K in Harvard Square. Cool! Two miles from where we lived. Actually, I think I saw this one before while we were having breakfast in Harvard Square. We would plot and plan for other races. I remember asking Alejandra if I could do a race the following weekend in Marshfield. She said, "No, you spend almost every weekend racing now and it's the whole morning, and then you are junk the rest of the day, no!" I said," But I love doing it, and it's good for me, I'm training and I'm seeing results. I need something to train for!" I ran the Tory Row 5K in just over 23 minutes. I want to see if I can get under 23 minutes. She said, "No. Enough is enough". She questioned if I was addicted to this. I wasn't in denial. I just told her I found a new hobby. I was addicted to this new environment, the new racing environment, the camaraderie, the atmosphere, the adrenaline, everything about it. I didn't really like running that much as far as training, but I reaped the benefits of it mentally and physically; it was changing me as a person. I quickly became a different person. Shortly after the GlassFest 8K running changed me for the better. I had a different outlook on life. I was more motivated, and it carried over to my work and my attitude too. I had this runner's high thing that gave me this burning fire inside. It was almost like the logs inside me were the void I needed to fill, I just needed to spark the fire. I was passionate about something now and finally had a hobby.

163

I told Alejandra again that I would need something to train for, and that I can't just run; it's just not the same motivationally for me. I had motivation but I was way more motivated if I had a race to train for, even if it's a 5K. I don't think she understood, and she still said no. Basically, I worked Monday through Friday and weekends were for family time. When I wasn't racing I would go for a run with Randy or by myself and typically over the weekend would go for a longer run, meaning like 6 mile 7 miles.

Chapter 30
<u>Forced Change Again-Laid off July, 2013</u>

From June of 2009 to September of 2011 I was an Assistant Food Service Director in Chelsea, Massachusetts. I wasn't super happy there and I was kind of complacent. I needed a change of scenery and I was eager to grow and have my own account. My District Manager had mentioned in one of our district meetings that one of the things that keeps him up at night is not having candidates to transfer to new pieces of business or to fill in or to replace other directors that might leave. He asked everybody to email him by the end of the day if they would be willing to be a candidate and be willing to relocate within our region. Once we left the meeting I got on my phone and sent him an email saying I was willing. The second day of school in 2011 they terminated the Food Service Director in Northbridge, Massachusetts. I was asked to go there for a week or two until they found another director. Then it was a month, two months; then they said you might as well stay till Thanksgiving. They saw that I worked hard, and they saw that I was a good fit for the position, so they asked me to stay for the year. That summer I helped out Chelsea Public Schools for the summer feeding program and then went back to my Northbridge account in the fall for year two as a Food Service Director for my own account. The district contract was going to be up in April 2013. Other management companies and mine had the right to bid on this contract and it's up to the district to choose a company, or they could go to self-operation. We had received word that one of our competitors had backed out, so it was my company and another company and they're going to make a decision in April. My company got the contract!

What I did not know was what was in the contract and what was bid on. I found that out in freaking July at a meeting with my District Manager and a General Manager. I had worked at the general manager's account for a month and got a lot of the district menus done among other things for the summer when school finished. In that meeting he told me that, as I know we received the contract. However, when we bid for the contract, we did not bid it with a salaried manager position. It would be an hourly manager and they would make $20 an hour. What did that mean for me? That meant that I was either going to have to find another position within my company or be laid off. I had a bunch of calls with human resources and recruiters, but nothing really panned out. I had a few interviews and for one reason or another, I got laid off. My new job was a stay-at-home dad. Which honestly was the best job I have ever had. How many dads have had an opportunity to see their young children grow up and spend that much time with them? This came as a shock but those were the cards I was dealt. What can I do about it? What could I change about the decision? Nothing. All I could do is to do my best to move forward and not dwell on the past. It was not my fault; it was just business. It's hard to make money in K-12. This contract they would be just breaking even with an hourly manager position. It was nothing personal, it was nothing I did wrong and I knew that. I gave a hundred percent and I slept well at night knowing that. It's called integrity.

I had a long talk with my wife as to what to do. I honestly do believe everything happens for a reason. Sometimes you don't agree with the reason or the timing of it. Sometimes we figure out the reason later. Timing for this was perfect. I just found running and now I can run more. I was burnt out from the industry and had been thinking about a way out for some time and possibly changing my career. I know-- maybe I'll make a career out of running? But how, or where? Work at a running store? Is there money in that? Is there money in the industry?

July, 2013

By this time, I was running probably averaging about 20 miles a week. I ran with Randy sometimes and he mentioned since he was rerouted in Boston back in April that he would automatically be running Boston next year. I asked him if I could run too. He said that you have to run for a charity or would have to qualify. Qualify? I thought I'd read that before, but this is kind of crazy, qualify? Yeah, so apparently many people want to run Boston and there are so many bibs, like 32,000 bibs, and you have to apply to possibly get a charity bib and then you agree to raise money for charity. What are the qualifications again? I have to run 3 hours and 15 minutes in a marathon in my age group? That seems kind of ridiculous and out of the question, now doesn't it? Especially because I had been only running for two months. This also meant I would need to run a marathon that would actually qualify me before September which was two months away. I had not run more than around 10 or 11 miles before. Oh well, I'll just run for a charity. What do I have to do? I really want in! When do the applications come out? Basically, fill them out and tell them how much I want

167

to pledge? Well, pretty much everybody in the world wanted to run Boston this year to show that unity. This year the demand was like no other year. Charity applications open up in late fall. First things first; let's run a half marathon.

BAA Half Marathon

I was told that the Boston half marathon, which is put on by the BAA, the same organizers for the Boston Marathon sells out pretty quickly. They have like 10,000 bibs that sell out in 12 minutes. We have to be online and ready when the date and time comes. I had it marked on my calendar. I set an alarm and made sure I was online and I was able to register. I remember sweating and being super nervous, not about running the distance, but whether or not I would be able to register in time. When the page refreshed and I submitted the payment, I was in! This was huge for me. They had a training plan set up on their website that I followed pretty much to a "T". Except, if it said to run 10 miles I would run 12 miles. I would run a little bit more and push myself. I learned about tempo runs, I learned about intervals, and recovery runs.

For those of you who are not runners, intervals are a type of training that involves high intensity workouts followed by low intensity ones. This increases your level of fitness faster. The easiest way to determine proper tempo pace is to add 24 to 30 seconds per mile to your 5k PR. The result should be about the pace you would be able to sustain for a full hour of running without needing a break. Typically, tempo runs are about 20-30 minutes in length and should NOT feel like a race at any point. At the beginning of the workout your breathing may seem labored. But as your body adjusts to the pace you should begin to feel as if you are running fast but in control.

The advantages of utilizing tempo runs are numerous. Notably, running at a sustained, hard pace for a long period of time builds endurance. Tempo runs train your cardiovascular and muscular systems to better deal with fast paces over longer races. Those who lack endurance often struggle in the middle to late stages of racing. Recovery refers to letting the heart rest and allowing the lactic acid to subside and not build up. I loved the training and being strict about it.

Back up to when I started running, my body changed and started craving things that I put in my system changed, too. My body started craving things like granola bars, yogurt, smoothies, berries, bananas. I wouldn't put anything in my system the night before a run or the morning of a run that would not agree with me. For

169

example, I wouldn't eat hot dogs because they give me heartburn and no energy. I wouldn't eat fast food. I probably would not eat a bacon cheeseburger. I started feeling better because the new me was healthy. Food is fuel.

9-7-13 Prospect Bandit Run 5K

I ran a couple of other races over the summer but toned it down. Family is the most important thing to me so I cut back on the amount of 5Ks I would register for. This Prospect Hill one was going to be first for me because it was up the steep road and then on trails to the top of Prospect Hill, down on the trails, then down on the road and back. Back in the day, we often drove to the top, hung out there and partied a lot, I mean a lot. We'd walk around the woods but that's about it as far as exercising there. We spent a lot of time at the very top taking pictures of Boston while smoking weed and drinking beers. There are no hills around besides this one. It was close to impossible to run to the top of it without stopping because of the steep grade. I asked Randy if he could show me that racecourse so we could practice. The first time we went there, we actually saw Tim Irving, the race director, putting up signs. After running for about thirty seconds, I was already gassed. You're breathing in the swampy humid air from the wetlands and eating bugs left and right. They are flying directly into your eyes, ears and mouth. What's there to like about this? It sucks all the way up, and then it levels off of it and then you try to recover your breathing and your legs and then you go past the gate and hit the trails. The trails are fine for a few then it becomes more technical. There are rocks

170

and tree roots sticking up everywhere I'm pretty clumsy so I'm really leery of this. I'm not scared, I'm just not that agile and it's nothing I've ever done before. When you are almost at the top, there are some friggin' rock stairs that are super steep. After you cross a campsite you are back on the steep road to the top, and then you start going down some more rock stairs. It's pretty steep; one false step you're down and out. Then it's down that steep road and you grind it up to the finish line. What a complete suck fest. I would say this was the most advanced course I had been on.

As I was running, I was questioning my sanity and was regretting registering, feeling I may have bitten off more than I could chew. What am I doing here? I have no business here. We did the same practice run the following week with the same results. It doesn't get any easier! This was very humbling, as I thought I was a lot stronger of a runner, but this was a different animal... Meanwhile Randy and Tommy put together a dream team of strong runners and he actually asked me to join the team. What a great honor. I'm on the same team with Jill and Brian Wilder., Randy and Tommy and a couple of other people. Wow. Team awards were given to the teams with the lowest cumulative average. We were the Waltham Wussies. We were there to win. I was a bundle of nerves as I didn't want to let the team down. But what I didn't know was that I was more ready than I thought I was. A lot of this is in the head and I quickly realized that. I took it easy on the way up, which was the advice from some other runners I talked to before the event. Just do choppy strides and then save everything for the straightaways and the trails and the way down. That's what I did. It still is really, really hard to climb, then run hard, then to recover and run again,

171

especially for a newbie. Going up those stairs on the top I thought my chest was going to explode and I was going to die. I was at max heart rate, which meant I gave my all and left everything on the road and on the trail on the way up. I had to recover and had to get my breath back but after I did that it would be pure grit and determination to the end. Just like that tailgate trot, I ran as hard as I could going down and did pretty well. Waltham Wussies placed second! I felt like I belonged and could hang with the big boys, and girls!

Chapter 31

Obsessive, Compulsive, Addictive New Habit

My training continued for the BAA half, and I used 5ks as my speed workouts to gauge where I was at with my speed, finish times, and compete level. I was hooked on the racing, and now the training as my finish times kept coming down and I was getting faster. Early in the summer, I would convince myself (and I honestly believed) I would win the race I was racing. I guess it was a false sense of hope, but it helped me to push myself, work hard and compete at 100%.

I still was looking for work, and still thinking about changing careers to my new passion. I was not having luck, so I did my best to live in the moment and make the best of it. I remember applying for positions that I didn't even want; there were no positions in my industry that I wanted. None. I was burned out. Like I said before, everything happens for a reason, and when the time's right things will fall into place. God has a plan' things do not happen on my terms; they happen on his. I learned in recovery to accept the change and embrace it. I learned it is not always what Henry wants and when Henry wants. God, grant me the serenity, to accept the things I cannot change, the courage to change the things I can, and the wisdom to know the difference. There it is again! What could I change? I cannot force companies or recruiters to call me or email me back. I can keep trying, I can keep looking, I can keep an open mind, I can network. I knew I needed to work; we needed to pay the bills. When the time was right, I would get that phone call or email. That I knew.

173

"Running helped me deal with life on life's terms."

I am thankful to have found running, or did running find me? I will talk about this in a later chapter, but my personal trainer instructor, Ron at NPTI asked me (and the class) if we found our sports, or did our sports find us? Think about that for a minute. For me, I think it was a little bit of both. What I do know is that the timing was right. I started running when I was 43. Better late than never, and it is never too late. Prior to distance walking and then finding running, I was a squirelly mess at times. I was driving myself nuts. If all of a sudden, I was laid off and had no hobbies, and not found running, would I have gone insane? Would I have pushed my wife further away? Running helped me deal with life on life's terms. Running made daily nuances and problems manageable. If I went for a morning run, most days the day would flow better. My attitude was better. If I was not having a great day, or felt overwhelmed, going for a run 99% of the time helped give me an attitude adjustment and different perspective. I had learned tools in treatment, now I had another powerful tool to add to my support system. Running.

Running teaches you to stay in the moment, if you do it properly. You cannot worry about what is going to happen in mile 22 if you are on mile 4. All you can do is worry about how you are moving right then and there, and not to fall! So many things can happen between mile 4 and 22. Worry and focus on the now. Worry about where you step and plant each foot, so you do not hurt your foot, or fall. Step by step, moment by moment.

I mentioned before about the running community on how cool the people were, and how welcoming. I was instantly welcomed, no

174

matter my checkered history, no matter my if I was an addict or an alcoholic. Just like AA, there was no judging. In fact, a significant amount of the runners that I ran with also were and are in recovery as well. Wow, I thought this was amazing. Runners are kind of like cult members, but a good kind of cult. I believe a lot of us are a bunch of misfits, at least in the ultra running community!

I started running with the Waltham Trail Runners and started meeting new people each run and Meetup. I always looked forward to these runs, to run with members of the community, pick their brains, and push myself. The same day I became part of this group, Sebastian also became a member by default. Being a stay-at-home dad, if I wanted to run, I needed to bring the little guy! I was known as the guy with the stroller. We started doing 4-mile Monday night runs up and down Prospect Hill. I had to bring Sebastian! He loved it, and people loved seeing him. He was such a good kid, and honestly, he was pretty lucky to be able to see the world from the vantage point of his stroller! All he needed was milk, gummies and stickers and he was a good little boy! We really looked forward to the weekly runs. These were my friends now! Every Monday, sometimes Tuesday, and sometimes Saturday mornings we would go run and chat. I met and made friends for life. People would ask how I could push a stroller up the steep hill, run the technical trails with the stroller, go to the top, and down? I said it was great training, and if you can run a hilly course like this with a stroller, a flat 5k was easy! And that was the truth. The next spring, my 5k times kept going down, into the low 20's. I really enjoyed running with Sebastian and knew that this was only a period of time, and I better soak it up. We enjoyed some longer runs over the weekends which I will talk about in a few.

One of the more memorable early runs that I had was with Randy. I asked him if he wanted to meet up and at our place on the Belmont/Cambridge line and run into Fenway Park around the park and come back, which is a little over 9 miles total. I had Sebastian with me in the stroller, we started out, we always had a great conversation and always shared some laughs. Next thing you know, we went over the Boston University bridge and were minutes away from Fenway Park. At that point I realized that there was no suffering and that we ran the four and a half miles or so pretty much the entire time without stopping. This was the first time I actually felt progress in this distance, and it became relatively easy. We looked around, took a few pictures and then made our way back and did the same thing without stopping. We did somewhere around nine and a half miles and this was a huge breakthrough for me. It wasn't the distance; it was just the lack of stopping and then also focusing mentally. When you are distracted, when you would have somebody engaged in conversation and you're not focused on the "this sucks; I hate this, this is hard, this is boring, my feet hurt, how many miles do I have to go crap" that we get stuck in her heads, it can be enjoyable and go by quickly. Time flies when you are having fun. That was just enough for that day, but I felt that I could have gone much longer. He gave me the confidence for the Boston half marathon for sure. The body will follow the mind. My mind was ready--just a little bit more training and I was there, too.

BAA Half

"I knew I needed to shut the evil voices off in my head"

I am not going to go on and on about every race, including this one but this was indeed a huge milestone. 13.1 miles. I ran most of my training miles pushing Sebastian, including a couple of 15 milers, oops I went too far! I was ready for this! Mentally and physically, I was ready. I was fine through the first four miles, and then I saw the elite runners COMING BACK!!! This was an out and back course, and these men and women were flying back. Unreal. I knew before it started that I would not win this one, but I also knew I would do well, I knew I would finish, just not where and when. Ironically, the turnaround point was mentally and physically the turning point for my race. I was not out of gas, but I knew I had started off too strong. Yeah, that NEVER happens, right? I started feeling bummed out and was thinking negatively. I thought a little about all the hard times I had growing up, I thought about the rough nights boozing, I thought about the guilt, I thought about how many tougher days and nights I had back in the day. During the BAA Half, I really tapped into the hard times and started feeding off it. "If I could get through those hard times back then, some tired feet or tired quads are NOTHING!" STFU and push through; you are not hurt. Most of the people out there were suffering as well, right there with me. At the time, there were 25 million other American actively suffering from addiction. I am doing something I supposedly enjoy; STFU, run and finish this thing! I started applying this mentality to long runs and events and I believe these hard times made me stronger and better prepared me for a battle within myself in a race, or tough run.

177

Chapter 32

Can I Make a Career Out of My Running Hobby? Visit to Corning October, 2013

I went out to visit our friends Enrique and Maritza. I had the time because I was still unemployed, and I wanted to shadow them to see what it's like to own a business and see what it's like to own a gym. One of their personal trainers was an ultra marathoner. I really had no idea what ultramarathon was. There's a guy from Waltham named Ken Doucette. I remember Ken had run a few ultras and was currently training for his third. It was told to me that ultramarathons are anything more than the traditional 26.2 miles. I assumed that it was more than a marathon but I just didn't know the distance or anything like that. It's not that I wasn't interested, but who the hell would want to do anything more than a traditional 26.2 miles anyway? The personal trainer's name was Mike, and he said he used to run a marathon every Wednesday night on the trails. Well, WTF! This guy is a badass. So I asked him the question: what is the definition of an ultra marathon? I literally looked it up after coming home but I wanted his take on it at that point. He said typically it's 50k and up. There are 50 milers, 100 milers, various different mileage events in between; 24-hour events, 72-hour events, 48-hour, seven days and there are also stage races. That's just crazy. Why would anybody want to do this? He talked about Leadville, about Badwater and a few others I don't remember. This is way beyond extreme, like Navy SEAL extreme.

"I started thinking about the Boston Marathon...I could do this."

I started bugging out on it. I had never run a marathon, yet and at that time marathon distance was my only focus. Wow, how inspiring to know that people push their bodies way beyond their comfort zone and there is something further than a marathon--wow, just wow. I enjoyed my time out there and then came back and started really ramping up my training miles and thought more and more about the Boston Marathon. I started thinking more and more about the distance. I could do this.

Chapter 33

The Cannoli Run- Enjoying my Long Adventures!

One cold and blustery winter Saturday morning, I bundled up Sebastian and geared up myself and we left with a plan to run to the Museum of Science along the Charles River from home and back. The total distance was 14 miles. I had done this a few times and it's relatively flat, but it still is 14 miles. This distance was by no means routine for me yet. As I stated earlier, I always like to go a little bit farther than my projected distance and start thinking about food. Once we got past the hatch shell, I started thinking about cannolis for some reason, and my mind went directly to the North End. The North End is a historical neighborhood that's predominantly Italian with the most wonderful food in the world! It's one of my favorite places on this earth. People say, "Where's a good place to get something to eat in the North End?" The answer is clear-- go anywhere! So, the body started following the mind and the stomach and my body would be going farther than ever before on foot to 17 miles. We passed the Museum of Science and made our

179

way past The Garden and the Bobby Orr statue, and then down Commercial St. and then next thing you know we were on our way to the North End. WOW! I had rollerbladed and biked here many times, but never ran here; this was so cool. I remember going up one of the hills to the right and barely being able to push the stroller up, as it was so steep.

Then I started smelling the smells and made my way down towards Bova Bakery. All I could smell was bread, pastries and delicious sauces that were simmering on stove tops in the various restaurants in the neighborhood. Wow, I made it to the North End and with Sebastian! I was in the middle of the North End. The doorstep of Bova Bakery is pretty steep, and I remember struggling to pick up the stroller because my legs were pretty tired. Then I had to open the door and lift the front tire and the back tire and get the stroller into the door without the back of the door hitting me in the calves and I finally got in. I'm starving. The plan was to get a half a dozen chocolate chip cannolis and bring them back home. My plans changed. I ordered those and when the woman asked me if I would like anything else, I said, "Yes. Can I have this loaf of bread? Can I have a pound of proscuitto de parma sliced very thin? Can I have a spinach and cheese arancini? Can I have a sausage, pepper and onion calzone, two slices of pizza, piece of cheesecake? Oh, and two of these M&M cookies, two of these and I think that's it. No wait--two of these, three of those, four of those..." $85 later, with a stroller full of food weighing about 30 pounds, I attempted to leave the store the same way I came in but my hamstrings were pretty much shot. I was struggling to get outside the door until someone held the door for me and then I stood there and ate a cannoli. It dawned on me now that I have to go all the way home. Basically, it was about eight and a half to nine miles there. My previous PR for distance was 14 miles and now I'm going to do at least 17 miles total? I had no strength left in my legs. It just dawned on me all at once--how am I going to get home? I thought about calling Alejandra, but she would not drive to the city unless it was an emergency. Was this an emergency? Not yet. But potentially.

Well, the cannoli kicked in and I told myself to just run as long as I could, just take it easy, especially with this heavy load. I gave Sebastian one of the cookies, which he
made a mess of as he held it in his grasp for about an hour! He was happy and I enjoyed watching him. I went back the same way I came. I don't know if you've ever been on the Charles River bike path, but it always seems like there's a headwind. With the extra weight, the wind up my face and the cold air beating me down, it seemed like I was going nowhere fast. I did a walk /run ratio and just kept moving forward. I knew eventually I would get there! Once I got off the river, I had a mile and a half until home. Once I got towards the house, I called Alejandra because I would need help getting the stuff in the house, as well as help with Sebastian and the stroller. As I was making my way onto our street I was overcome with joy. I started thinking that was pretty hard, and was glad it was over, but I would definitely do it again. My prize for finishing was well worth the struggle and the journey, I had earned all these wonderful groceries from the North End that I purchased and brought home in the other stroller. Hence, the cannoli run was born. Once I started telling people what I did it became a thing. I took

countless running friends on the route and did the same thing with them. I actually started a blog: Will Run For Cannolis.

Here is a part of my blog and an example of one of my epic Cannoli Runs!
https://www.blogger.com/blog/posts/4090278291871369918
What would you do for a cannoli? How far would you be willing to run? Would you run 16,17,18,19, 20 miles for cannolis? I would.

When I used to drink, or use drugs, I would do stupid, insane things. For example, On several occasions, I went 20 miles to Billerica to buy a 24 pack of cans on a Sunday (liquor stores were not open on Sundays) on my FRIGGIN' ROLLERBLADES. I would put them in my backpack and fall home. Running into Boston for cannolis is much safer.

While living in Belmont,MA, I would test my endurance and sanity, by going farther and farther, never really following a traditional training plan. I was new to this running thing. A lot of my running in my first year (2013) was done while pushing Sebastian in his stroller. I was laid off, and a stay-at-home Dad. It is frowned upon to leave a 1.5 year-old home alone to go running... If I wanted to run, I had to bring my little training buddy!

Now, as for my cannoli run, it wasn't the easiest run home. Run/walk/stop repeat! I made it, and felt amazing after, and had all this lovely food to enjoy! I then started doing more of these, and in

182

time had built up better endurance, so it became much, much easier. Now it's routine! I have taken several runners along on this silly little run, but it's something people don't forget. Most runners love to eat, and who doesn't love a cannoli, or 12?

So, no stroller tomorrow, as Patrick Caron and I will be leaving my house in Waltham, MA by 3:30AM. My alarm is set. I grabbed ziplocks to hold 6 cannolis each, laying them flat; then I will wrap them in a towel for cushioning and place in my ultra pack. For the record, Bova Bakery is open 24 hours: bovabakery.com We'll go the looong way and get in 26-30 miles for sure!

Ready to go. It's 3:33 and Patrick and I are off. I'm pretty tired; didn't a great night's sleep, but whatever, no turning back now. We ran with a flashlight in the dark, all the way into Boston. We decided to go directly to Castle Island to see the sunrise before hitting the North End.

We stopped at Bova's Bakery on the way back. Good call, as it started to get hot out. You can't keep cannolis exposed to the heat too long, or they would be turned into smoothies.

We took the bike path along the Charles River in and out. Nothing particularly exciting happened, just great conversation, business ideas, running talk and conversation about life in general. I used to run away from my problems. Today, I look for solutions, and talk

185

about them, without dwelling on them. Running is a great way to chat with someone.

Though my diet is fairly clean, I do enjoy my sweets every now and then. There are a lot of people who are recovering addicts and alcoholics that have found running. Granted, it's a new addiction. I definitely have an addictive personality and need to be aware of that. I once ate 9 cannolis and I couldn't open a bag of Doritos without finishing it...I was hooked on running from the get-go. I need to be careful. My first year I wanted to register for every race on cool running. I need to remember that family is first, running is second. That's why I am willing to run at 3am, so it doesn't interfere with my family time! Today I brought home 3 cannolis, which I will share with my family. It's 9:30AM, I ran a 50k and have the rest of my day enjoying my family, high on endorphins from running. And cannolis, too! I hope I can share one of these cannoli runs with each of you.

Chapter 34

Full Marathon- December, 2013

The December issue of *Runner's World* magazine featured marathons around the country and around the world. I am now obsessed with running marathons. I knew that I could do the distance and fully understand a lot of it is mental. After I ran that 18 miles on the cannoli run, I ran 20, 21, and 22 miles a couple of times. It was hard but I knew that if I could do that, I could do a marathon. I applied for three different foundations and hoped to raise funds on their behalf for the 2014 Boston Marathon. I had a few connections and so did Randy, and I thought for sure that I would get accepted to run for one of the charities. A couple of the applications took 45 minutes to an hour to complete. You had to write why you wanted to run, what connections you had to the cause, how you feel about running and how you were going to raise your funds. I think the minimum at the time was $5,000 to $7,500 per foundation, and since so many runners applied, they really weren't taking anybody that didn't pledge less than $10,000. I think I pledged $7,000 and needless to say, since they had so many applications, it took a long time for them to get back to everybody. Unfortunately, I was not accepted to any of the charities for 2014. I was disappointed, but I knew that it wasn't personal. But I did know that I still wanted to run a marathon.

I started dissecting the *Runner's World* Marathon Edition. Being unemployed with little income I know it wasn't great timing to go on a runcation. However, I like to think I'm pretty crafty and perhaps maniacal at times, I knew I could figure out a way to make

187

it happen. Maybe if we did a road trip--maybe, if we went to a city where we knew people, and maybe if we packed food it would be cheaper. I started thinking about all this and decided I wanted to go to Pittsburgh. I've always been a Pittsburgh Pirates fan and I have always wanted to go to Pittsburgh in general. It was a 10-hour drive, Sebastian was really good in the car and we love our road trips, so to me this was logical. One Sunday morning I got on the computer and just started going through the Dick's Sporting Goods' Pittsburgh Marathon website. It was ranked in the top five marathons by *Runner's World* and pretty much sold me.

I started looking at the foundations and quickly realized that I could just pay for the marathon with registration. Wait. I didn't have to qualify for this marathon, I could just pay the $150 and run? Then I thought if I'm doing something big to challenge myself, why don't I raise funds while I'm doing it? There were about 50 different charities. So, I looked through them and found one called Urban Impact. Urban Impact is a charity that helps children and families in the Northside of Pittsburgh. This is their mission statement: "Our mission is to do our part in fulfilling Christ's Great Commission on the North Side of Pittsburgh by following His model of holistic ministry by investing in the lives of at-risk children, youth, and their families in order to develop responsible followers of Christ." Through their church and through sports they have helped thousands of families in need. Some of the funds they raised went to building baseball fields, basketball courts and helping with educational programs. The funds give the students and children something to do after school to keep them busy and with the intention of staying out of trouble.

188

I decided to see what this application process was like. The minimum to raise was $600. With Boston, you have to put it on a credit card. If you say you're going to raise $10,000 and you only raise $100 you're on the hook for the remaining $9,900. Urban Impact did not ask for a credit card and $600 is a lot easier to raise than $10,000, even though I never raised more than $100 in my life. Well, the application process went something like this: Name, address, phone number, email, confirm email, emergency contact, emergency contact, phone number, shirt size, initials, finish. Next thing I knew, the page refreshed and said: "Congratulations, you are now registered to run the 2014 Dick's Sporting Goods' Pittsburgh Marathon." Well, I got a lot of explaining to do. Alejandra had said I could run a marathon, just not yet. I was obsessing over it and really wanted to do it and I mentioned Pittsburgh to her somewhere between 50 and 100 times. She kept saying, "No, wait until you have a job." My argument was that we never have time and money at the same time, and now we have the time. If I can figure out the money can we go. Please, please, please, please, please, please!

I told her I had registered that Sunday morning--after walking around on eggshells for about 3 hours. The honest-to-goodness truth is I didn't realize that I was actually registering. I thought the process was too simple. It took me two minutes to do, unlike the Boston Marathon application. I thought for sure I'd have to get an interview, get accepted or something like that--but next thing you know I was registered. I don't know if she believes me to this day, but that's the truth. For a couple of weeks, it was kind of in limbo. I had a very nice phone call with Cindy who is the director of the program. Next thing you know I'm 100% in and raising funds for the first time ever. I could not wait to tell people, especially Randy and Tommy, that I was registered for my first marathon. I was already looking forward to long training runs with them, as they would be continuing their training for Boston, and I would train for Pittsburgh!

Pittsburgh Marathon: May, 2014

The Pittsburgh Marathon was all that it was cracked up to be and then some. I can't say enough great things about Cindy Dell and Urban Impact, about Pittsburgh as a city, about the Marathon. I liked it so much I came back the next two years. No, I didn't qualify for Boston. I had a really good finish time of 3:33 and learned a lot about myself. Just like in life when you think you're down and out you can't come back--and just like that Boston Half Marathon I felt that it was hard-- just not as hard as I thought it would be. I envisioned it being kind of like I saw the Boston course growing up spectating. I envisioned possibly collapsing, having cramps, crying, then eventually crawling to the finish line dragging one leg. I ran the Boston Marathon course as a training run and took walk breaks and stretched too, especially the last five or six miles. My plan was to do a certain pace and then take it easy on the hills going up. All that training pushing Sebastian up and down Prospect Hill was going to pay off and then I would just absolutely fly down the hills of Pittsburgh. The Pittsburgh course is pretty hilly; I knew that, and I studied the elevation on the map. The problem was I never really practiced running downhill. When you are running with a stroller, your shoulders can be elevated and your arms are straight. I had no problem generating energy without my arms. But what I did not practice was running in proper form going downhill. With every step I took my quads took a beating. It felt like someone hit me with a sledgehammer. My pace diminished and then when I got to mile 24 which was kind of flat and that's when I really suffered and got sloppy. I learned to keep pushing through the pain. I knew that I wasn't injured just because my muscles and my body were working harder than they probably ever worked before athletically. All I could do was the best I could at that moment and keep repeating that for the final 2 miles. The voices in my head kept saying, "Never doing this again; check this marathon thing off the bucket list, I am one and done."

After I finished, I had the thoughts and "what's next." I enjoyed traveling and wondered if we could have more runcations, maybe once a year or something. At the time I didn't realize it, but I quickly got the marathon bug. I started thinking about which marathon I could do next. After speaking with Enrique, a question came up about running the Wineglass Marathon in Corning, New York! This would have been my second marathon and Enrique's first full marathon. We had a place to stay with our great friends. Our kids can play together and spend the whole weekend enjoying each other's company while the guys can run the marathon! Time: I bettered my marathon time but was still two minutes shy of qualifying for Boston. You still need to be under because so many people apply. I mean really, you need to be 3 to 5 minutes under.

There was a podcast company called Pace Per Mile hosted by Chris Nicholas. They had a weekly contest that gave away one free registration to any race that wasn't sold out. You could not choose a lottery race, or one you had to qualify for. I enjoyed following them and listening to them and my name was selected for a marathon! I got to choose any marathon I wanted which was pretty cool. Chris was actually at the Boston Expo and I did an interview with him during my first year running. Chris was also at the finish line of the Wineglass Marathon the next time after that, so we shared a few moments, had some conversation and did a quick interview. He asked me which marathon I wanted to do. Out of all the marathons in the country I chose the Arizona Rock and Roll Marathon in January of 2015. This would be my second time going back to Arizona. We made the arrangements, got the tickets and we would be going back to where we used to live, back to where I got sober, back to where my distance walking really started, and now to run 26.2 miles. I ran by many places where I used to drink heavily, many places I visited and places that I worked at. The emotions were certainly raw during this race and I was doing really well. The wheels fell off the bus around mile 18 when my IT band started acting up and that caused my right leg to come to a screeching halt pretty much every 2 minutes. Then I would have to walk it off and start running again when I could. (For those of you who are non-runners, the IT band runs from your hip to the side of your knee. It flares up from overuse and the feeling will linger if you don't take care of it. It's an annoying pain. Rest, cycling and cross training can strengthen your legs and your glutes to relieve the pain.) It was pretty disappointing, but it is what it is. I did the best I could and just kept moving forward. I felt alive, I felt connected to this state,

192

and I still love running the distance. I had thoughts about moving back here during and after the race, but I knew the timing wasn't right, yet.

Runcations and Other Marathons

In March of 2014, Tim Irving scheduled a half marathon and called it the Bandit Half. It was old school. He had a stopwatch and a clipboard on his truck and then we ran 13 miles through Lexington, Belmont, and Waltham. It was really, really, really cold and windy and I was hating life while running it. I remember thinking I want to finish as fast as possible so I can be warm as fast as possible. I took off like a bat out of hell and every time I turned back, I did not see any of the runners. I wrote down the directions because I could get lost in my own driveway! Every time I looked, I was on track and I was going the right way. I drove the course a couple of times just to make sure I knew where I was going. The turns were marked with cones at key points. Every time I looked back there was nobody. There was a water stop about half the way and when I got there everything was frozen, so I had little to no water. When it is really cold like that you don't need as much, so I just kept going. I remember seeing Kathy Irving near the Shell gas station and she told me that I was in first place and doing well. She asked me if I need anything and I said no, I just can't wait to be finished. When I finished there were no crowds, no finish line or anything like that-- just the clipboard, the timer and a pen. I finished in first place, holy shit. There was nobody there to greet me. It was a great feeling but so weird! I ran as hard as I possibly could the whole entire time.

193

Just like other races I went in with the mentality that I would place first. I was not cocky, arrogant or anything like that--just that was my mindset. I was confident. I always have plan A, B and C. Plan A is to win. Plan B is to do the best you can, Plan C is to dig deep, crawl, scratch and claw the way and just finish.

July 2015 Coventry Marathon
"All the hard work paid off."

I posted something on Facebook and asked if anybody was doing the Coventry Rhode Island Marathon. This was part of the New England race series and not an official qualifier, but it was a marathon and only 45 minutes to an hour away from home. My friend Roger Wright said he was running the race and wondered if we might want to commute down together. I don't think I've ever met Roger until that day, but we immediately hit it off and shared a lot of laughs along the way. He is pretty inspiring. You can check out his story here about overcoming adversity, significant weight loss and perseverance. https://youtu.be/Ja9BFx5Mhqo This was a crazy course, as you had to do 20 laps to complete the marathon. Each lap you did you went up to the scoring table and grabbed the rubber band and put it around your wrist; when you grab 20 of them you turn them in and then you are done. I kind of had a feeling I was in the lead and I ended up winning this marathon. With my time of 3:19, I had finally gotten way under the 3:25 I would need to qualify for Boston. All that hard work paid off. All the things I learned about the other marathons that I did also paid off. I played a smart race in which my splits were consistent. (Splits are segments of a race; a mile or a kilometer. Splits can be either good or bad –if

194

you start off wrong.) I was onto the next marathon, The Erie Marathon in Presque Isle, Pennsylvania.

Erie Marathon 9-13-2015

Just like anything, I never want to get too high or too low. I was feeling pretty good about this marathon. My friend Joe and I both registered and I drove with him to Presque Isle. For anybody that doesn't know this area, it seems that any storm that's within a hundred miles will hit the Great Lakes area and hit it hard. We had some torrential downpours and heavy winds on the way down. As we got closer it got worse. We went to the Expo splashing through puddles and it was still pouring out. At the Expo, they sell shoes, jackets and nutritional items. They also have speakers. This was the afternoon before the marathon. I think really all we did was check into a hotel room, then we got something to eat at night and we didn't move around that much besides going to the Expo really quickly. Between that and sitting in the car I probably developed a lactic acid build-up. It may have been my downfall. We got up the next morning and much to our surprise, there was no more rain after one hell of a stormy night. There are a few puddles but nothing major, and the race was on.

I felt good at the starting line. It was windy but nothing too crazy. I put my music on and then when the gun went off it was time to go. Like most races I started off too strong and I found myself huffing and puffing. I looked down at my watch, and I was doing six-minute miles with the rest of the pack. I had no business starting off this fast or running with them, so I slowed down. They say if

195

you think you have started too fast, you probably did. I did. After the first mile or so I slowed down to get my heart rate down and then at about mile 3 I started to feel pain and fatigue in my left quad, then pain in my right calf, then pain in my hammy, pain in my feet and pain in my hips. Everything was kind of seizing up on me. I never really get sore, especially during a race. I had never experienced this before in my life--what the hell's going on? My first thought was, "Oh my God I'm never going to qualify for Boston!" "If I feel like this now, how am I going to feel at mile 15, or 20, or 22, 23, 24? I might not even be able to finish this!" I did some body sensing and determined that I was not injured. I was just kind of beaten up for some reason. I didn't think that it might have been because of sitting in the car all that time and not moving around because of the weather. But that probably was the case. Regardless, what could I have done about it right then and there? Not a damn thing. All of a sudden, I had these overwhelming voices in my head telling me to stop, to quit, to cheat, to turn around; this is not your day. All this negativity was killing me. I could not stop the voices. I had to shut the music off. I couldn't listen to anything. I needed to really concentrate and figure out a way to do this or figure out if I wanted to stop. I would never cheat, or ever quit. But I really was in a considerable amount of discomfort. I knew I wasn't injured but what the hell, I had to go 23 miles like this? Why would anybody want to do this; why would they want to put themselves through this? Maybe there is something wrong and I just don't know about it yet? I've never experienced anything like this; there has to be something wrong, but what is it? After some more assessing the situation, I just said I'm not injured, I'm just sore and I can push through it. I've been

196

through more pain in my life, especially during active addiction years. A lot of the pain was mental, but mental pain can be worse than physical pain.

"I just kept telling myself to shut up and run and finish the race. I blocked out the negative voices."

For 23 miles I basically just kept telling myself to shut up and run, shut up and run, shut up; don't listen to the voices in my head, shut up run, shut up and run, shut up and run and finish the damn thing. My finished time was 3:29 minutes. I hated this race but I'm really happy with my performance. I learned so much about myself, about running, and perseverance. This race was one that made a difference. I was able to block out all the negativity for basically 3 hours with non-stop chatter in my head and just pounded through the pain or found a way to keep going and finish. As they say I was comfortable being uncomfortable. I made friends with the pain. It felt like every step I was getting punched in my quads or kicked in my shins, but it was almost like getting a tattoo or a deep tissue massage. It's kind of pulsating so it's like pain for 2 seconds, gone, pain for 2 seconds, gone. It was kind of rhythmic and I got used to it. Once I finished, I had a great feeling of relief but also one of great satisfaction. That race gave me confidence to get through other things in life and other races down the road. I missed qualifying for Boston, but I gained much more---the ability to deal with pain. It's important to understand your body and know when you're injured or you're just uncomfortable.

Chapter 35

Transition to Ultra- Run to Work From Home

It may have been that sitting in the car and not moving around too much causing lactic acid build-up were my downfalls for the Erie Marathon, but it could have been over training too. In 2015, I started running more and longer. I wanted to get to the point where if an opportunity came up I could run a marathon at the drop of a dime. My goal was to build up my running base. In other words, I wanted to build up my endurance and strength. I was going to Best Fitness in Chelmsford, Massachusetts at least once a day lifting weights, taking spin class and some other classes too. A spin class is a form of endurance training that lasts an hour. It's a high intensity workout with music on a stationary bike. It helped me get stronger as a a runner by building up my legs without the pounding of running. It is mentally challenging as you keep pushing yourself. Quite often I would run there, take a spin class and run home. I started asking my questions about ultrarunning, I joined a couple groups on Facebook and made some new friends quickly, most of whom had beards and enjoy drinking things like Tailwind. I started learning more about some of the big ultra marathons and what it takes to run them. It was very intriguing to me. I also started early that summer running to work every Wednesday. I think I ran to work 12 weeks in a row every Wednesday. I would leave my car at my parents' house, which is a mile from my work, on Tuesday with a protein drink along with a change of clothes. Alejandra worked kind of close by, would scoop me up, bring me home and then the next morning I would drop Sebastian off at daycare and then take off with my pack and water and run 20 plus miles to my parents' house in Waltham. Most of the time, I would go the long way and get 26 miles. It may have rained for Erie, but I set myself up for something bigger.

It left me hungrier, and I now knew really how to deal with intense pain. Between going to the gym for spin class and doing these weekly long runs I was building up some great endurance and I was practicing running on tired legs. A lot of sports, especially running, are mental. You have to put in the time physically but it's the mental skills you have to hone. I mentally had to push through to get to my parents' house in time to get a shower, grab my protein drink and go to work down the road. Sometimes I was running behind and really had to push on the tired legs to make it on time. Another key was recovering quickly. I needed to be on time for work, be alert, productive, and be able to be on my feet! I would put in between 20,000 and 30,000 steps on average at that job per shift!

M2M-Manchester To Monadnock Ultramarathon

As soon as the registration opened up for the Pittsburgh Marathon 2016, I registered on the first day to run on behalf of Urban Impact again. I wanted to make this a tradition after such a great experience the first year. Then, I found out about this website called ultrasignup.com. Ultrasignup is like cool running but on steroids. This is where you find all the ultras! Most of them are trail races. I did some trail running, but I was mostly a road runner. I was up for a new challenge. One Saturday morning I was scouring through ultrasignup and I saw this Manchester to Monadnock Ultramarathon and it was free! I'm like, really? Manchester New Hampshire to Mount Monadnock is that what this is? I registered, took a leap without hesitation. Oh my God, what have I gotten myself into now? What have I committed to? There was a guesstimate number of miles, somewhere around 50, holy shit. Well, I had to start somewhere, and this was a progression to the marathon distance. I will figure out how to train for this. The next day I got an email from Bill Conley the race director. He said he always wanted to do this route and decided that he would put the route on ultrasignup so he and his friends could run it in somewhat of an organized event. Then he quickly realized that this is a race, as 50 people had registered, and he had to stop the registration there because his email was blowing up! People actually registered for his little fun run or fat ass event that was just a pipe dream! And I was one of them. Bill said he didn't want to let anybody down, and this was going to happen. He got the permits, and it was a go.

When I registered, I did not look at that calendar, because if I did, I would have realized M2M was 13 days after the Pittsburgh Marathon! How the heck was I going to do both? I figured let's continue just to practice running tired. That's what endurance and ultrarunning is all about, right? I will use Pittsburgh as my final long. For marathon distance, a marathoners final long run usually is 20-22 miles. I would use 26 miles as my final long run for the 50+ miles I would run for the ultra distance. All I could really think about was Pittsburgh and M2M, especially M2M. I didn't want to

200

overlook Pittsburgh, but I was really looking forward to doing my first ultra. I had no idea what I was in for!

3-25-16

By now, I had run 12 marathons, and done that distance or more maybe 50 times. I was really comfortable for that distance and wanted to know what it felt like to do more before I got myself into this M2M. Numerous times I trained on the Boston Marathon course, including running from Hopkinton to Boston in its entirety. One day, I thought how cool it would be to start at the finish line, then run to the start line and then go back to the finish line and do a Boston Marathon double or a yo-yo, whatever you want to call it. An out and back of 52.4 miles and completing two marathons consecutively. I remember being in great spirits leaving the finish line and then heading past Kenmore Square; then once we got to Brookline and then Chestnut Hill, I quickly realized that this is no joke. Going backwards and going uphill most of the way while reversing the Boston course was no fun. Negativity did not creep in, but the self-doubt did. Why would I want to do this and why did I decide to do this?

In ultras it's okay to walk, especially on the hills. This allows you to conserve energy and if you can walk faster than you can run at that moment, why would you run? I practiced using short, choppy strides to get up the hills or just power walked really quickly--then got through those hills and it was a little bit better, but I had to go all the way to Hopkinton! That's where the starting line of the Boston Marathon is. I still needed to run all the way there and then

201

turn around and come all the way back to the finish line. I practiced staying in the moment. I was ecstatic to get to the starting line. After taking some photos, it was time to head back to where I had started. I had no idea how I was going to get to the finish line! Once you stop sometimes and then try to start up again your muscles can tighten up and that was the case for me. My energy level also was lower as I had no clue how or what to eat besides Swedish fish! I have a weak stomach from traumatizing my body for years and was really reluctant to put anything into my system during a run. Now I know why I had a lot less energy. My glycogen stores were pretty depleted, and I needed to eat food. Food is energy, food is fuel. I lived off Tailwind and the fish for this one!

Having my friend Roger with me was a huge help. He was concerned that he would slow me down! I think I was slowing him down. I was just grateful to have him by my side. We have the same kind of wacky sense of humor, sarcastic and dry sometimes and shared lots of little jokes together and just basically talked about silly things which passed time. He helped distract me and I was not dwelling so much on the suck. Roger and I have shared many memorable runs like this, and this one was epic and no different. We did a walk/run ratio, eventually made progress to the cities and towns and ultimately wound up in Boston. Towards the end, I was pretty tired, and I was satisfied with this run for sure. This gave me the confidence that I could do Pittsburgh and then M2M 13 days later, as it was a testament that the human body is pretty incredible. He started telling me about the year before that he went out to seek David Clark and some other people that were

202

doing something similar to my Boston double. David was doing "the quad." I asked what the hell is a quad? Quad means "four." David did four consecutive marathons on the Boston course and the official Boston Marathon was his fourth. What? I was certainly okay with just doing two marathons back-to-back. This was a pretty good accomplishment, and I was satisfied with my efforts. This was a truly remarkable journey and I really enjoyed doing these long adventures, taking pictures, documenting and making memories.

Chapter 36
Runwell- October, 2016

Runwell, www.runwell.com the Linda Quirk Foundation is a movement; people coming together to provide accessibility of resources to those needing recovery from addiction and mental illness, helping people live healthy, fulfilling lives. We believe partnering sports with addiction treatment helps to keep individuals, and their support bases, committed to recovery. Runwell awards grants to fund existing scholarship programs and support-based training programs that offer effective treatment, empowering those affected by addiction to choose recovery and begin healing. Runwell is committed to engaging families and communities in the recovery process, believing that addiction is seldom won alone.

I had heard about Runwell through Facebook. I had a friend named Chad Moye and David Clark was an actual Ambassador for them. I had followed David's journey of recovery from addiction and saw some of the crazy things he was doing, which was super inspiring and motivated me to do more. I honestly didn't realize that he did this quad thing until Roger told me, but I knew he did a 24-hour treadmill fundraiser and other major fundraising things for Runwell. So, I reached out to Chad and asked him about his experiences with Runwell. I looked at Runwell online and liked what I saw. It would involve sharing my story of recovery and hope with them and with the world. I would be applying to be an ambassador. There was a link on their site for how to help or to run one of their signature races, or you could just make general donations. I saw some of the

204

Ambassador spotlights. A lot of them started leading group runs from recovery centers, and some of them ran larger races such as the New York City Marathon and raised money and awareness. I thought to myself, I could raise some money and possibly run a marathon for them. I ran and raised money for Urban Impact; I can certainly do the same for people in recovery from addiction. I could relate to that because I'm in recovery myself.

I filled out the application online to become an ambassador. I got a phone call from Michael a day or two later and we hit it off. Michael was in charge of the ambassadors, the marketing program and the fundraising. We both agreed Runwell would be a good fit. However, I was unsure how I would help. I did know that I could do something for them, and it would be a good partnership. I filled out a short bio but was hesitant to share too much about my darkest days and my recovery in general. My bio was pretty short and sweet and to the point. I started telling people that I was running for Runwell and wearing their shirts; however, I didn't have a plan. I reached out to a couple of recovery centers and hospitals in the area, but nobody seemed to want to work with me to start a running program. I thought it was kind of weird. I was going to offer my time for free to show people a healthy lifestyle and how to run, but there was no real interest. So, what should I do with Runwell? I had a bunch of races already lined up for the year. I was already raising money for Urban Impact and The Pittsburgh Marathon for the 3rd year in May. I'm running Manchester to Monadnock after that. Financially and timewise, I'm probably not going to be able to travel for any more races this year so what am I going to do with Runwell?

205

Sri Lanka Virtual Stage Race on the Treadmill: February, 2016

I love being outside and running outside; no matter what the weather was, I would still run. Just like the postman would, through rain, sleet, snow, whatever the weather might be, I just like being outdoors. What I didn't like was running at 4 in the morning when it was dark with black ice everywhere and running where the snowbanks stick out in the road. I had to keep stopping to let cars pass by because there's no sidewalk. Between not being safe and not having any place to run it became super annoying and unsafe. One Friday night, I decided to go to the gym with Alejandra and I hopped on the treadmill for the first time ever. Actually, it was the second time; the first time was when I tested out some sneakers, my first pair of running shoes! The second I started running I felt like I was going to fall off the thing. I really hated it. I think I almost went insane as well...

February 14th, 2016 was my second time ever running on a treadmill. The first time was the night before. I would much rather be running outside. I was sitting in the Best Fitness parking lot waiting for it to open and saw a post from my friend Chad Moye. He had introduced me to Runwell in November and was about to be running his first marathon. I asked my wife if I could run virtually to support him. She said it was OK, but how are you going to do that? I said, "On a treadmill." The doors opened, I picked a treadmill and started walking. I put on some Slayer music or

206

something, and the walking turned into running. I thought to myself, how the F am I going to do this?

The stage distances are below:

Stage 1, 14 February: 37 km / 23 miles
Stage 2, 15 February: 39 km / 24 miles
Stage 3, 16 February: 44 km / 27 miles
Stage 4, 17 February: 46 km / 29 miles
Stage 5, 18 February: 30 km / 18 miles
Stage 6, 19 February: 50 km / 31 miles
Stage 7, 20 February: 4 km / 3 miles
TOTAL: 250 km / 155 miles

1st dibs on a treadmill.

Here's some of the thoughts that went through my mind in the first few miles. This sucks; I hate this and I am never doing this again; this is boring. I started looking for aches and pains, more or less excuses to quit. I really had no reason to quit. I committed to doing this. I had to do it. But how? I doubted the body would follow the mind on this one. I did start to get pretty bored, I have to admit. I had seen the highlights from Sportscenter four times by now. I was scrolling through my phone and noticed the founder of Runwell Linda Quirk, Walter Bortman and Patrick Bowles were starting Stage 1 of The Racing the Planet Sri Lanka Stage Race and they were running 23 miles on day 1. Perfect, I only have to run 23 miles on this stupid thing instead of 26--I'll do that! I will virtually run stage 1 of Sri Lanka! Well, I couldn't only run stage 1. It's ALL or nothing. I thought to myself, I can do this. I will do the entire stage race and ALL on the treadmill. I took a look at the other stages and wasn't sure I could find the time but committed to giving it a shot.

As I looked at Facebook, started reading more about this stage race and the rules online, I found out that they had to carry all their own gear except for water, including nutrition, sleeping bags, and a long list of mandatory gear. Holy shit! That's pretty badass. That is the ultimate Adventure! So, all three of them raised a bunch of money and awareness for addiction, packed all their gear and went out there to compete in a 6 day event. How cool is that? I want in.

Obviously, it's too late for this year but I wonder what next year's going to be? It said on their website that they are having the next roving race in 2017, and they will announce a roving location every other year. I wonder where the locations are going to be? Regardless of where it is, I want to go! I started obsessing over it. I remember texting Alejandra who was going to meet me at the gym with Sebastian and asked if it's okay if I could run 23 miles on a treadmill at the gym. She was like ,"What, you just said you were never running on a treadmill again. Last night you said you hated it?" I said, "I know but...I decided that I would support them and do the stage race virtually on the treadmill!" When I say I'm going to do something I do it a 100%

The actual distance to the first day was 23 miles. How the hell am I going to get to 23 miles on a treadmill? I knew I could figure out a way to get it done. I got to 2 miles and found some Swedish fish in my gym bag that were left over from Halloween! I used these little packages to bribe Sebastian into going to the gym with me. They had a daycare that you could drop children off for 90 minutes. Please do not judge, but if I wanted to work out sometimes, I would need to bribe him! I ate a few of them myself. This made me feel happy, and my thought process became more positive. Something changed. I decided that I would reward myself with a few fish every 2 miles. Every 2 miles was like an aid station. All I had to do was break this run down into 2-mile increments. Next thing I knew I was at mile 12. It's all in the head! Before I knew it I was at mile 18, 20, 22 and it was all downhill from there. The Swedish Fish tasted great and gave me energy from the carbs they provided, but most of all they distracted me, and it was something to look forward to. This further reinforced the fact that that most of this was in my head and this is certainly the case here. If you think it sucks, or if you dwell on how boring something is, it will suck and it will be boring. You will have a hard time and you may quit. If you wake up and say I hate my job, I don't wanna go to work today, my boss sucks, you will have a shitty day, no doubt.

I completed the 23 miles the first day and the next day was 24 miles. I was impressed with myself that I was able to stay there because I have trouble staying put in one place for a long time. 24 was the next challenge. I said if I got through 23 yesterday and I can get through 24 today. I did the same thing and rewarded myself every two miles with Swedish Fish. I had the same results and before I knew it, I was past the 20-mile mark and then I finished 25. The next day was 27, the following day was 29 and I think the day after that was 18. Then it was the death march of 31 miles, and the final day would be 3 miles, the victory lap! Once I got halfway through the week, I knew I would finish it. It was hard because I had to work too, so I was getting up at 2:00 AM and going to the other gym, which was open 24 hours. It's never easy getting up that early, but I wanted to get it done so that's what I had to do. I finished this virtual Sri Lanka 250 km 7-day challenge on a treadmill!

"I pushed through mental barriers and it made me a stronger person"

This experience changed me as a person. You can do almost anything if you put your mind to it. Breaking it down to smaller increments helped. I definitely pushed through some mental barriers, but I believe it made me a stronger person in the end. I

210

built up more mental endurance. This Sri Lanka virtual run planted many seeds. One, being the desire to run a 12-hour treadmillathon fundraiser, and another was to run the 4 Deserts 2017 Roving Race, which the location was announced as Patagonia. This race was in November 2017. I decided that I was not going to register for that many races the upcoming year, only a few larger ones. Guess what, I registered for Patagonia.

http://www.4deserts.com/beyond/patagonia/

I couldn't stop thinking about when the registration would be open and when they would make the announcement for the new location of the next roving race. I signed up to receive the "Racing The Planet" newsletters, I reached out to them and stayed in touch with the powers-that-be at Runwell. They knew I wanted in! This was my calling. This was something to train for. This was what my intuition was telling me I needed to experience.

"Telling people about one's story of recovery is a way of giving back"

In March they announced that the location for 2017 would be Patagonia, Argentina in the Andes Mountains, which is one of the most remote, beautiful places in the world-- an adventurer's heaven. After going back and forth back and forth with Alejandra I told her it was really, really important to me. I really wanted to do it. I knew I could do it. I knew I could raise the money and this would be a life-changing thing for me. I finally registered and it was now time to put a game plan in place, not only for the training but for the fundraising. Kim Pawelek had taken over from Michael at Runwell

211

as the program director. I had some email correspondence with her and then a telephone conversation. She immediately became a mentor to me and gave me courage and guidance that got me started on this journey. Linda Quirk, Kim and I talked about fundraising and marketing. Linda encouraged me to expand my bio on the Runwell page and share it on Facebook. We agreed that I had a following already and people needed to know that there's life after recovery. I was hesitant to share my story previously, especially publicly on Facebook. I'm not afraid of being judged. It's just that I personally did not have conversations with some of my close relatives and a lot of my friends. They didn't know that I was in recovery and what I went through. I thought it wasn't their business and I would tell him when the time came, just not publicly on Facebook out there in the open. After some deep soul searching, I felt this was super selfish. Telling people about one's story of recovery is a way of giving back, which is what we are supposed to do. We should show people there's hope we can recover; it would be selfish for me not to share my recovery story. It might encourage someone suffering to seek help and get into a treatment center, give them the courage to change. Getting somebody into a treatment center is ultimately saving their lives. How cool is that? So, I expanded on my message of Hope. People who are addicts or alcoholics don't want to be the way they are, and I certainly didn't either. There is nothing to be ashamed of but I was ashamed of some of my actions. It wasn't my fault I was an addict or an alcoholic. So why not share?

By sharing my story, it opened up a lot of doors for me, but more importantly I got a lot of positive feedback. A lot of people have thanked me for being brave and courageous and openly admitting I have a problem. Other people ask me how to get help themselves or for their loved ones. It was pretty cool. So I had a fundraising page and updated and shared my new bio. Now it's time to fundraise. I feel like when I fundraised for Urban Impact that I was hounding people. I was asking the same people for the same funds for the same reason. I feel like I didn't go about it the right way sometimes. It's hard to raise funds if you feel like you're nagging somebody, especially if I said I would remind someone or someone said to remind them, I would follow up and follow up and follow up and I still would not have a donation. I hated that. I was obsessing and bothering people at the same time. I spoke with Kim and just reminded her that I knew I could make an impact. I knew this was a good fit and I would come up with some out-of-the-box thinking when it came time for fundraising.

"I wanted to make a difference in the world; this was my calling."
The first thing I did was set up a fundraiser for Runwell at my gym Best Fitness in Chelmsford Mass. I decided to do a 3-hour spin-a-thon there. It was a perfect collaboration. Best Fitness held a Health and Wellness Expo and I held a 3 hour Spinathon at the same time. I was still raising money on behalf of Urban Impact for the 2016 Pittsburgh Marathon and now I'm raising funds for Runwell too, which was not easy! The Pittsburgh Marathon as usual was a great experience. What an amazing city, and Urban Impact as usual was really good to me. It was great to see my team, Cindy and her family. The plan was to run for Urban Impact and run The Pittsburgh Marathon for eternity but plans changed. I'll talk about

213

that later, as we ended up making a decision to move to Arizona. I think I raised around $1,500 for Urban Impact and raised around $1,000. For the first time, I got to share my story for an event, and it created a lot of dialogue about addiction, recovery and treatment. This was just the tip of the iceberg though. I knew I could do more for recovery. I saw what David Clark and some other people were doing around the country and the world, and I knew I could do some of the things they did. I had tough shoes to fill but I knew I could push myself and my body to do great things. I wanted to make a difference in this world; this was my calling.

The actual spinathon was interesting. This was a particularly stressful time in my family's life to begin with. On top of that a couple days before the Spinathonon, our dog Luci was throwing up a lot. She went from never sick, to very sick. We thought that maybe she just ate some grass or picked something up in the woods that didn't agree with her. She was eating very little so since she was throwing up anyway, we just gave her water or chamomile tea. She became a little more lethargic and not herself so we said we'll keep an eye on her; it will pass. We had made a decision, which was a tough one, to put our townhouse on the market. We were 20 miles further north from my parents, Alejandra's work, my work, and where we spent most of our time. In retrospect, Alejandra was not enjoying that distance. It just was not a convenient location, plus, it never really felt like home. After we made that decision to put it on the market, a day later we had a bunch of offers that we could not refuse. Now what? Where are we going to live; what are we going to do? We were in limbo, so we weighed out our options. We decided on the Friday night before right before the Runwell

Spinathon we would go down and talk to my parents. The plan was to ask them if we could stay with them for a month or two until we figured out where we wanted to live. We would put most of our stuff in a storage unit and then basically just bring our clothes and the belongings we didn't want to put in storage and stay with them.

When we got home at 9:30pm I opened the garage door and went up the stairs and Luci, who always greeted me, did not greet me. I remember putting the light on, hearing her collar and then I heard kind of a thump. I started walking over to her and she collapsed again. She was just kind of lying on her side and I remember screaming, "Oh my fuck*** God, my dog is dying." Alejandra just said, "She's not dying, she's just sick, don't jump to conclusions." Why do I have to deal with this? Because things do not happen on Henry's terms, this is part of life. We Googled "animal hospitals open 24 hours near Chelmsford, Massachusetts". We found a place in Westford, called them, grabbed a bed sheet and picked up this 65-pound dog, put her in the bed sheet and like a sling or a hammock. We carried her down the stairs, put her inside the back of the SUV and drove her directly to the hospital. They were there waiting for us. They helped Luci out of the car and into the hospital and ran an IV. An hour and a half later we were sitting in the waiting room when they told us the first diagnosis--that she's not doing well and she has some sort of major liver issues. They were very nice there and proceeded to tell us the various costs of overnight, the IV, the cost for 24 hours and everything that they could give us for options. It was going to be $1,800 per night and they wanted to keep her for seven nights. They can't tell you which decision to make but they did say that the chances of her still living

215

were not very good, and also helped to answer questions about the chances of her living a healthy life. The odds were not very good. Without doing extensive testing they felt that she probably had liver failure because her liver enzymes were really high. It was 1:00 AM and the night before the Spinathon. I had to make the difficult decision to have my dog Luci euthanized. We got to say goodbye. We felt that since Luci would not live a healthy life, we did not want her to suffer. She was never really sick and had a good life up to that point, but it was super sad obviously to lose our family pet. Going home and trying to sleep was close to impossible. I may have gotten one or two hours of broken sleep.

"Once I turned everything over to God, the urge to drink disappeared. "

I needed to get up and think about doing the spinathon. Physically getting through a spinathon is not that bad--it's mentally more difficult, and with this just happening was a complete mind fuck. The first half an hour I remember thinking about Luci and kind of dwelling on it, feeling sorry for losing her and feeling sorry for myself. I was not fully engaged in the event that I created. I just wasn't into it; my body was, my mind wasn't. Then something clicked. I knew that I needed to be present; recovery taught me to live in the moment. I needed to make peace with what happened to Luci only hours before and just be present for my own good, for my own sanity. I remember saying a bunch of Serenity prayers and just praying to God that I could be present, and it worked. What could I do about Luci's passing now? Absolutely nothing. I stopped dwelling on it. I started enjoying myself and I was engaged and before I knew it the event was over. This was a powerful lesson for me, and just another example that God is good and that being present and not dwelling on the past is a good way to live life. In

216

recovery, we are supposed to leave everything up to God, and put things in God's hands. I wouldn't be here today if it were not for God, and having faith in God. I know that it has been proven over and over again that if we have faith, things usually end up turning out better than imagined. I could not quit drinking or using on my own, but once I turned everything over to God, the urge to drink disappeared. God guided down the path of sobriety and created miracles over and over again from me. If I keep putting the work into sobriety, I can be of service to God as a messenger to others who are suffering from addiction.

Chapter 37

12 Hour Treadmillathon 2-18-17 Corning, NY

My 12-hour treadmillathon was part of the road to Patagonia. I already committed to running The Boston Marathon Quad on April 1st, which is the Boston Marathon course 4 times. More about that later. These were both fundraisers for Patagonia.

https://www.facebook.com/events/1904803219755299/?ti=cl

https://www.facebook.com/events/240355413056954/?ti=cl

I was invited by our friend Enrique, who owns a Snap Fitness gym in Corning, NY (where my running career started) to do this event in their gym! I am running for Runwell helping people who are suffering from addiction to get the help they need by getting them into a treatment program and get them into running. "Changing lives, one footstep at a time." I ended up raising over $2,000 and I was able to reach a larger audience because the media had picked up my story. This was the first time I was able to be in the news, on radio. This event, my story and running gave me a platform to share my message of hope that we can recover.

http://www.mytwintiers.com/news/local-news/12-hour-treadmill-a-thon-to-help-fight-addiction/659235913

218

You will never win treadmill!

I ran the 1st 50 miles in my Luna Monos.

April 1st I will be running the Boston Marathon Quad for the 1st time, Boston Marathon course 4 consecutive times.

Chapter 38

Next Stop, My First Ultramarathon: Manchester to Monadnock 5-1-16

In truth, I had no idea what I was in for, yet I was both physically and mentally ready for this. The 3-hour spinathon was the week before and really helped me get my mind prepared. All the cross training in the gym, all the mountain biking and spinning classes complimented my running and made me stronger. I often would go for a long run, then go to spin class and then run home. Practicing running when you're tired hardens the mind and builds endurance.

I remember showing up feeling like the new kid in town on his first day of school, shy and timid, just kind of standing back. I had met a couple of the people that had registered through Facebook but we had no interaction except for the night before at the little expo we did at the church. I saw them, chatted it up a little bit and put my mind at ease before the race started. Just like any other race, once we started running, I had to check myself to see how I felt--whether I started off too strong or not. I was in the front of the pack for the first eight or nine miles on the trail feeling very comfortable with that. I didn't feel like I started off too strong as I was running and chatting with some of the other runners. Next thing you know, we went from running flat to having to go up and over Mount Uncanoonuc. It is only 1,324 ft but it is steep. The stronger runners that I ran with in the beginning, most of whom climbed like mountain goats, were gone--never to be seen again by me! I practiced like I was running up Prospect Hill, but this is a little bit different. Maybe I did start off too strong; maybe it was the timing

222

of the climb. I power hiked it, got to the top and I was alone; I took a few pictures and started down the hill. Road marathons are so much easier to not get lost!

There are aid stations sometimes every mile or every other mile and the courses are often lined with cones or flags or barriers as well as people along the roadways. This had none of those things. This course had yellow arrow stickers on the roads pointing us in the right direction and little orange flags that said M2M on them along the trails. As I went down the mountain there was supposed to be a turn-on to a skimobile trail which either wasn't marked, or the flag was missing, or I didn't see it. When I got to the bottom of the hill I had to turn around because I stopped seeing flags, and it's like what the F! What an awful feeling! I'm lost. I had written down directions I made on an armband that NFL football players would use, indicating turn-by-turn directions and mile markers. The last thing I saw was "turn on skimobile trail, follow to whatever road was next." As soon as I started backtracking, there were two other runners there, Dominic and Michelle. They were both lost as well, so we backtracked together and never found the skimobile trail. I showed them my directions and we all had cell phones so we could find a way out of this mess together. I was so happy to see them because I didn't have cell phone reception right there. I have a very poor sense of direction--I get lost in my own driveway! We decided that since we cannot find the skimobile trail that we head out to the road and try to get some sort of a cell phone signal. I immediately thought of this as some sort of reality show and we're basically on this island with little to no resources and left to fend for ourselves, which was kind of cool. I finally got a cell phone signal.

223

I knew the crossroads where we needed to get to so we plugged it into Google Maps, put walking directions, started going that way and we walked up this hill and down a little bit. Then we quickly realized that we were walking the wrong way and had to turn around and head down the hill, back up the hill and then we were finally on our way. We were 3.3 miles away from where we needed to be, what the fuck. Why did this happen to us? We lost so much time when we had been doing well. I think we were probably all somewhere around 10th-12th place and now God only knows where we are. Probably everybody passed us. What the fuck, this sucks! Dominic and Michelle both ran several ultras before.

I knew there was plenty of time to make up and it was very early in the race. My mindset had to switch to put getting lost in the past. It was over and done with, it was a mistake, we need to learn from it, we cannot dwell on it, there's nothing we can do about it now except move forward. And if we kept dwelling on it, that negative mental abuse would end up eating us alive and potentially make us drop or at least suffer miserably with all the negativity. "God grant me the serenity to accept the things I cannot change, the courage to change the things I can and the wisdom to know the difference." We could not change anything that had happened, and we needed to move forward. We made a pact and with the exception of laughing about it later, we committed to burying it and moving forward. We found the trail that came off the mountain as we saw runners filing out one by one. Five or six of them all said, "Hey, where were you, what happened? Weren't you way ahead of us? "Long story short, we got lost." We exchanged pleasantries and talked a little bit and then the runners dispersed. Dominic was having trouble with his

224

knee and I ended up giving him my little neoprene knee brace thing I had, and he told Michelle and I to take off without him. It was hard for me to do because I thought we were just going to run together almost like a security thing. He insisted that Michelle and I keep going. Michelle and I immediately hit it off. It's like we knew each other already, which was really cool. I immediately knew she was a certified badass, but when she said she had to go to the bathroom right on the side of the road in the woods, that was a whole different level! I asked, "Hey, can you just do that?" She said, "This is an ultra; where else am I supposed to go!" Good point, this is so crazy awesome. We were doing fine. The course was tough for the next 40 miles up and down some steep roads through lovely Southern New Hampshire.

Every step after the first 27 miles was uncharted territory for me. I had never run more than 27 miles. Every step I would be going farther and farther and farther. We went 50K. I remember shortly after the 50k distance, the wheels started falling off the bus a bit. I fueled myself with only Tailwind and watermelon. I thought I was in great condition and prepared for the hills, but the hills on this course chewed me up. I was in a considerable amount of pain, as we were probably on our feet for 8 hours by now. Michelle told me it was okay to walk. In fact, we could walk faster than we could run so why not save the energy and just walk? We power walked and this proved to be beneficial because going up the hill you can really stretch out everything including the hips and my legs, which actually would help me recover a bit and feel better. Once we got to the top of the hills, we would gently run down and run the flats as long as we could and then walk again. We just kept doing that until he got to Mount Monadnock. It seemed like forever to get to the top of it, but we did it. I remember being so depleted at that point, just wanting to be done and I did not want to take any pictures, I just wanted to go down!

Going down, my legs were shaky at best, but I knew that without a shadow of a doubt, we would finish. We basically had fewer than 5 miles to go on this course but we were still on the mountain. I was beaten up like I had never been beaten up before in an event. I was mentally and physically exhausted, finally got down off the trail of the mountain and got to the fire road which was runnable. We had not been running for a few hours between the mountain and then walking up the last couple hills. I assumed a few hours ago that we would not be running any more for this day. Once we got on that fire road, adrenaline kicked in and I don't know what happened. We didn't talk about running or anything like that, but all of a sudden we both were just running, and I was like, "Holy shit, we are running, why are we running? Oh well, it feels okay!" All the pain and fatigue were gone, blood was rushing into our bodies and we were going to finish. We pushed and pushed and pushed and probably had our best mile splits the last mile or two. We were actually running harder than we had all day. I decided with about a half-mile to go that we would finish together. We started this thing together and we will finish it together. Most races, especially in ultramarathons, the odds of running with somebody else--especially a complete stranger for that long were not good. But we were pretty much at the same fitness level, and we bonded. Sometimes you might find somebody else who might be at the same fitness level but they could be annoying, they could not talk enough, they might talk politics or for one reason or another you stopped to go to the bathroom, they kept going or you your pace diminishes, they kept going or vice versa. But we're on the same page; Michelle and I are going to finish at the same time together and that's exactly what we did. In the process I made a friend for life! I stayed around the finish line for a little bit trying to wrap my head around what actually happened. I finished 54 miles with a time of 14 hours and 7 minutes. The first ultra was complete, and I got the bug, the ultra bug. I went from, "I'm never doing this again to what's my next challenge, what's my next ultra!"

"Established on such a footing we became less and less interested in ourselves, our little plans and designs. More and more we became interested in seeing what we could contribute to life. As we felt new power flow in, as enjoyed peace of mind, as we discovered we could face life successfully, as we became conscious of His presence, we began to lose our fear of today, tomorrow or the hereafter. We were reborn."

Alcoholics Anonymous

Chapter 39

What Else Can I do With Runwell?

At this point, I still hadn't really FULLY shared my story publicly, especially on Facebook more than once or twice. The dumbest thing was that I did it just to get it off my chest. I am still running for Runwell, but I'm just not sure what I will do with them next. I mentioned before I always liked the adventure part of running, so I started doing more and more adventurous long runs and taking pictures along the way to document the insanity. I was connected with a group of people's teams for beach the beach, so I had this idea of doing this solo reach the beach thing or a "fat ass" run. I reached out to my friend Michelle who I ran M2M with. We left my house in Chelmsford, Massachusetts and ran all the way to Salisbury Beach! I thought afterwards that this would have been a great (missed) opportunity to raise funds.

When I signed up for Racing The Planet Patagonia Stage Race, part of the deal was the benefit of having a professional running coach. And mine was Lisa Smith Batchen. Her coaching and friendship made all the difference in the world in my training. I had just gotten the word that she was going to be my coach when we had an initial interview and the first thing she asked me was, "Do you want to be running when you're 80 years old?" I said yes. She said, " Good, because we are going to be doing cross training for injury prevention to make you a stronger runner. Are you okay with that?' " Yes, of course! "She had asked me what I did for cross-training. I told her about mountain biking, weights in the gym, spinning class and walking. She asked me if I ever did tire pulling. I said no, but

228

I've seen the videos--in fact I saw one with Linda Quirk tire pulling. So, the next thing you know I ordered myself a tire trainer from www.trailtoes.com . If you have never tried tire pulling you haven't lived! It's basically like a weight lifting harness you velcro around your waist that is attached to bungee cords attached to a tire and you pull it. It teaches you to use your core and your trunk and teaches to use your hips to move forward. You have to engage your abdominal muscles and your glutes to pull this thing, which is what you're supposed to do when you run. This made me a stronger runner for sure. Lisa asked if I had any more questions. I said, "Yeah, just a couple." I told her I like going for a couple of really long runs during the week and wondered if that would still be okay. I have a friend Patrick, who joined me doing long runs on Tuesday mornings and sometimes on Saturdays as well. If not with him, I went with somebody else and then mixed in some other distances during the week. I asked if it was okay to do one or two long runs like I was doing was Patrick. She said, "Yes, of course. I actually waited for my training plan to arrive via email. When it arrived I noticed that the first day she had me running 35 miles! I was blown away by this. We have a deal! Needless to say, Lisa helped shape me into the runner that I am today and certainly helped prepare me for some of the races that I did-- especially Patagonia, Badwater and Cape Fear before that.

Running Alone/Speedy Patrick

So, I kept posting on Facebook: "Does anybody want to go for a long run at 3:00 AM on a weekday?" Go figure--all I got was crickets. (Silence, that is.) Well one of my character defects of

229

being an addict and an alcoholic is obsession. I started obsessing over it. Why doesn't anybody want to go for a run? Why would they not want to go before work? You get the long run out of the way and you have the whole day to ride that runner's high and propel you through your workday or your school day. But nobody would bite until one day when I put that same thing out there. Does anybody want to go for a long run on some random Tuesday in the middle of July? I got a response from Patrick Caron. He said he would run with me. I said okay, sure, I'll be in touch. I looked at his profile and remember the only interaction I had with him on Facebook was when I was thinking about doing a hundred miles run from Nashua, New Hampshire basically to the Bourne Bridge into Cape Cod and he had indicated interest in that. I didn't really know who he was; he was just a Facebook friend. I looked through his Facebook page and then Googled him and I was like holy crap, this kid ran like a 14-minute 5K and he ran Boston the year before in like 2 hours and 43 minutes. He's pretty fast; oh, and he's 18 years old--what the hell does he want with me! At the time I remember being intimidated and thinking I'm old enough to be his father-- more than old enough to be his father. But I had asked if anybody wanted to run with me and he was willing to do so and at 3am on a Tuesday morning!

The following Tuesday, there was Patrick outside my parent's house at 2:55 AM! I went outside and said, "What's up? Good morning; how are you doing?" All that good stuff. We had tentatively talked about doing a long run, and that's exactly what we did. The first time I ran with Patrick we ran from my parents' house in Waltham, Massachusetts through Belmont to the Charles River,

230

took the bike path into Boston and eventually went to Castle Island, around it and back and got in exactly 50k! Pretty crazy! We hit it off from the get-go as we talked shop, about running, about life in general. Not only did I find a new running buddy, but I found another friend for life. Patrick was a straight-A student that pretty much could have gone to any college he wanted to but was at a crossroads. He wanted to do something with running and fitness. He would tell me about his ideas and his vision, and I would tell him my ideas and I would share my visions. We talked about some of the ideas for what I wanted to do with Runwell. His running ability and his speed far exceeded mine but if you want to get faster, I suggest you run with somebody that is stronger and faster and knows a lot more about it than you do. He was like a mentor for me that was 18 years old and I was 45 at the time. Many Tuesdays we did our long runs. It sometimes included trails of the Western Greenway and Prospect Hill of Waltham, Massachusetts and sometimes we would even include a track workout at Belmont High School with Becca Pizzi and her group. If he could not run on Tuesdays, we would pick another day during the week and then sometimes even on Saturday. At this point in my life, I was running an average between 80 and 110 miles a week, which was by far the most miles in a week. People including family members asked me why I was running so much. I even heard: "What are you running away from? Don't you spend time with your family?" And then the usual comments: "Don't your knees hurt running? It's not good for you" and all that good stuff. I did it because I like the way it made me feel and I did it to keep myself sane.

231

We had insurmountable problems at the time. There were family dynamics and critical health issues to deal with. It was the second most challenging part of my life. I felt that I needed to run to help me deal with life's problems with a cool head, on life's terms and in a calm manner. Running helped me do that; running helped me move forward and tackle them one at a time. Running was critical for getting me through these hard times. At this point, many friends and family members still didn't understand why I had to run so much. Also, I had a training plan for a stage race in Patagonia in November of 2017. If I didn't put the training in, I would be doing a disservice to myself, Runwell, Coach Lisa, and to everyone who was struggling with addiction that was suffering worse than I was. All or Nothing, All In or nothing, and that includes training. Honestly, my training was going better than ever.

Becca Pizzi and The Belmont Track Club

I believe that people come in your life at the right time. This is certainly the case with Becca Pizzi. I was friends with her on Facebook and for those of you who don't know her, she's in the *Guinness Book of World Records* for the World Marathon challenge. Pizzi finished an average of an hour ahead of all four of the other women competing in all seven races. Her cumulative time of 27:26:15 hours (an average time of 3:55:11 hours) was declared a world record for the event.

I went to Moozy's Ice Cream to buy some ice cream and there she was sitting there. I looked over at her, she looked at me and we

232

made eye contact. I said, "Hi, hello, we're friends on Facebook."
She said, "I know you; you're the guy that runs all over the place!"
"Yeah, and you're the girl that runs around the world!" So we
talked for a few minutes and then she invited me to run track with
her and her group. At this point I would rather run a 50k distance as
opposed to doing any speedwork, but I'm an opportunist and I
believe that's what I was meant to do. I was meant to be at track
every Tuesday at 5:00AM. I showed up and it was life changing.
Every single person there was inspiring and motivated by others;
you could feel the energy. I hated the workout because it was hard
but when I finished, I couldn't wait to do it again. It seems like each
week it was humid, it rained or in the winter it was windy and
freezing cold, with snow and ice--but every damn week we showed
up. Early in the year I vowed to do things that I didn't necessarily
want to do. Speedwork was one of them. I immediately started to
reap the benefits as my 5K times were well below 20 minutes and
even below 19 minutes consistently. If you want to run faster, you
have to practice running faster! Go figure. The old cliche hard
work pays off--it really does. Week by week I kept showing up and
I actually loved it!

"At this point I just wanted to be the best me."

I ran a couple Race Around Waltham series races and then a couple
of other local ones and PR'd a few times including the PR (personal
record/ my personal running time) that I still have today: 18:35 for a
5k. At this point I'm really enjoying running. I'm enjoying the
progress and I'm enjoying the community. The shorter distance
races would now be used as speed work. I also enjoyed seeing
friends and people from where I lived. I've always been
competitive, but at this point, I just wanted to be the best me. I was

233

hard on myself, but I just ran how I felt with no pressure on myself. It solidified that a lot of this is in your head. While it's okay to analyze, you don't want to stress your body. If you waste your energy it can get you in a dark place, making you want to quit.

When people say: would you rather have more time or more money? I say both, but if I had to choose, I would say more time. I always wish I had more time to do the things I want to do. At the time I was obsessed with doing so many bucket list races, most of which were out of state--which meant either plane tickets or a long drive. I love to travel. I love to go on vacation and see different things, how different people live and try different foods. Traveling also kind of helps shape who you are. I wish I could spend my time doing runcations! I already registered for my first 100 miler which was the Javelina Jundred in the McDowell Mountains in Arizona. We were still living at my parents' house and in limbo about where we wanted to live. Arizona was one place I was thinking about. I wondered what it will be like to live in Arizona this time around with my new life of sobriety and running. The distance of this race intrigues me as it was more uncharted territory, but I knew I could do it. My intuition was that I was really going to like being back in Arizona. My intuition was correct, and I'll get to that in a little bit. All the miles that I was putting in week after week certainly paid off and I was ready for that event in late October. The first step was the Maine Marathon in Portland, Maine.

Chapter 40

Running Without The Devil/ Portland Marathon 10-2-16
Birthday 15th Marathon BQ (Boston Qualified)

We looooove to visit Portland. The food is amazing, it is easy to get around, and the city has a great vibe to it. I noticed the Maine Marathon was going to be held on my actual birthday, and Alejandra and I decided that a weekend in Portland would be a nice place to spend my birthday weekend.

My training was more than adequate, and my nutrition was as well, leading up to this weekend. I have to admit it, but some of my nutritional choices while we were in Maine were not the greatest. For example, fried clams, French fries, fried pickles, whoopee pies and Holy Donuts just to name a few. I did make sure these items were consumed before 2:00 Saturday and ate plenty of pasta Saturday night as FUEL for Sunday's race.

We woke up and hit the road to the starting line. No traffic, no problem parking. One of the things I liked about this race was that everything was low maintenance. No stress. The temperature was around 45 degrees and it started to mist a bit. I ran around a little to loosen up. Ten minutes before the start I lined up in the corral. It was really neat. For the first time ever in a race, there were bagpipes! Also, I looked up and saw drones. Another first---they used John Deere gator quads as the official pace cars.

Holy Donuts

The weirdest thing happened to me after the National Anthem was sung. I was very foggy in the morning to begin with, and all of sudden it dawned on me that I needed to run 26.2 miles. I had not really given this RACE much thought! Not being arrogant, I honestly had not. My Plan A was to run balls to the wall, enjoy myself and run the entire race. Plan B was to run hard, enjoy myself and do the best that I could. Plan C, just finish, and finish healthy. Other than that, I had not given it much thought! But there I was, about to run this thing. I just decided to look at it as a long run. After all it was going to be used as training for Javelina Jundred anyway. I had no pressure, nothing to lose, nothing. I decided to just run how I felt, and to just enjoy the run. So that is what I did!

I started off with 800 marathoners, 3,000 half marathoners, and a bunch of others doing the marathon relay. I fell into a nice groove from the get-go, and never looked back. From miles 4-6.5 I had

236

some guy who sounded like Darth friggin' Vader right behind me. I could not shake him. I moved to the left, and he moved to the left. I surge forward up, he surges forward. WTF guy! Heavy, obnoxious breathing. I thought about slowing down and letting him pass but did not want to disrupt my race and pace. I also thought that mentally if I let him pass it could ruin my groove and my mojo. Finally, I reached the half marathon turn around point. ALL I can say is that I am forever grateful that Darth Vader registered for the half! I don't think he could sustain his pace anymore regardless, but I was glad I no longer had to listen to him!

I still felt strong and wasn't even thinking about my time per se. I just recognized that my splits were consistent, and between 7:15-7:35 mostly. After mile 16, 17, 18, 19, 20 they were still in this range. When I got to mile 20, I knew if I could sustain this pace, I could qualify for the Boston Marathon! I always kept in my mind that things could go to hell in a handbasket at any time and reminded myself just to keep running the mile I was on. I got out of my own head and let go, just running how I felt. I stayed in the moment—just like sobriety.

There have been other marathons such as Wineglass, Arizona, and Erie where the plan WAS to qualify for Boston. For each of these marathons, I felt my training was adequate, or more than adequate to qualify. I put the time in, I was eating properly, I ran hills, I rested. After a difficult time running 23 of the last 26 miles of the Erie Marathon in considerable pain, I decided to rethink my goals. I hated this race. I was a mental case the entire race as well. I put too much pressure on myself and was not having fun. I always said from the beginning of this running journey that if I am not having

237

fun, then what is the point. I was physically injured for the Erie Marathon whether I wanted to accept that or not and tried to push through. All I ended up doing was running all banged up and overcompensated on the other side of my body, which caused both legs to implode in mile 3! I felt like quitting. I had to stop listening to music; I was a mental mess. I pushed through to see if I could get used to the muscle pain and fatigue, which I am glad I was able to do. I suffered, but I recall telling myself that I suffered a lot more many times when I was boozing...That helped keep me going. I rehabbed my ankle, took the foot off the gas on my training runs, and focused on cross training. Prior to Erie, I ALWAYS wanted ALL my runs, including long runs, to be under 8 minutes per mile. I broke down. I was not having fun. That is when I decided to run slower so I can go longer, and injury free. Intensity dictates duration. Less intense = Run forever! This was one of the best things I could have done. I also set aside my goals for qualifying for the Boston Marathon and shifted to an ultra running mindset.

I ran Baystate, Roxbury, CT, Hyannis, Pittsburgh and Mexico marathons just for fun. Do not get me wrong, I ran hard and just did the best for these races. But my expectations and goals were just to have fun, run hard, but finish healthy. If I just felt right, and just so happen to be in a position to qualify for Boston, then great. If not, then so be it. I also used these marathons as preparation for ultra marathons.

Qualifying for Boston—a Birthday Bonus!

Well, the Maine Marathon just felt right. Everything just worked for me. No internal issues, no muscle pain or fatigue, no tweaks, no heat, no wind. After mile 20 I was passing people who had passed me earlier in the race. One girl who I fondly remember was Holly. Holly passed me around mile 4. Holly had a friend on a bike pacing her the entire race. This was kind of annoying. The pacer would hand her a water bottle from her bike, she would take a few swigs and then just chuck it. WTF! Every 1/2 this was happening. She dressed the part of someone competing in American Ninja or Tough Mudder. She wore a bandana, straps on her arms, KT tape all over her body! I don't mean to make fun of people but.......she and her silly pacer were ultra-annoying. The pacer friend kept telling her she looked strong, looked good, all the typical cliche sayings spectators yell at marathon runners. They will say this even as someone has obvious distress. I saw someone yacking and someone still looked good! I got to mile 24, and was like, "Holy shit, it's Holly! I knew at this point that unless I totally imploded, I was in line to qualify with a little cushion of time. I passed Holly and her friend, which put a little more bounce in my step for sure. I still felt great, so I decided to run as fast as possible to see how much was left in my tank. Surprisingly, I was able to finish strong. I qualified for Boston. What an unreal feeling. I was just planning on enjoying my birthday long run, what a bonus!!! I think the key was just being loose, not putting any pressure on myself, and being healthy. For those that are trying to qualify, put the time in, and your day will come. A lot of this is between the ears... The key was quite frankly getting out of my own head!

239

Chapter 41

Javelina Jundred- My 1st 100 Mile Race October 29, 2016

After finishing The Maine Marathon I was able to put my mind at ease and I was ready to pack and get ready for our trip to Arizona. First and foremost, this was just an unbelievable and amazing experience. I doubt that I can describe how great this truly was. Despite the blazing heat, I really loved every minute of it. Aravaipa Running did an outstanding job organizing, marking and designing the course itself. This was not just a race; it was an experience and an event that has changed my life for the better. I will never be the same.

This being my first 100 miler, I really did my homework. I am truly grateful for the sound advice I received from veteran ultrarunners, and from my coach Lisa Smith Batchen. I probably used half the stuff I brought in my drop bags, but if I did not bring it, I would probably need it! The gear I did bring was spot on and worked well.

We arrived in Arizona on Wednesday, three days prior to JJ100. I figured I should probably get acclimated somewhat, because Boston was 35 degrees when we left. Besides, who would not want to spend as MUCH time as possible in The Valley of the Sun? We got settled in to our hotel Wednesday, and I got to organize my gear a bit.

240

GEAR!

Speed up to Thursday.... Sebastian, Alejandra and yours truly drove up to Sedona. If you have not been here, you are missing one of the single most beautiful places on earth. This is Red Rock Country. It's very peaceful and serene, and people often go here specifically for spiritual healing. I personally have never run here, ever. I have been here close to 20 times, but those visits were during the period of my life when I drank like a fish and had not even given running a single thought. This would be my last run before JJ. I left town and found the Broken Arrow Trail. Scored big time! This is trail porn to say the least. Single track dope, the most beautiful trails surrounded by red friggin' rock.

SEDONA PIX!

I ran and took photos for an hour, went back to town and ate lunch, grabbed Sebastian, and drove back to Broken Arrow! We certainly had a blast. His favorite thing was the dirt!

243

244

245

Thursday night we went home and stained the shower with red dirt-
-I mean, we took a shower at the hotel. We went to a friend's house
for stuffed shells, one of my favorites. It was very tasty and right up
my alley. Let the carb loading commence! Thanks Sam!

Friday afternoon, Sebastian and I did the expo and bib pickup thing.
I met some new friends, and finally met in person some friends,
David Clark and Walter Bortman. It was cool to hang out there and
soak up the good vibes. After that, I ate and went back to the hotel
early to get as much rest as possible. My alarm is set for 4:00 am;
the race starts at 6:00AM.

Up and at em'. I depart by 4;20! It took 40 minutes to get there, which was fine. It gave me enough time to drink my coffee and digest my Generation UCAN bars. I parked, and found where I was supposed to be, Jeadquarters!

Ace of Spades - I can power walk more than most
humans!

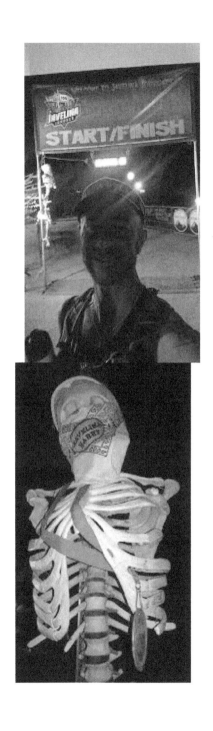

Runwell teammate Walter

**West's Best, East's Beast Teammate
Sandra!**

It is time to line up in the starting corral. It's 6:00AM and here
we go! Holy shit, we are off! Well, we didn't start off like a bat
out of hell; in fact we started off by literally walking the first
mile due to too many people on a single track. I was definitely
Okay with this because it kept my pace in check. Everyone I
talked to, and everything I read about this RACE said not to start
tooooo fast. I was able to start passing people after the first mile
or so, but consciously aware of my pace. I was averaging about
9.5-10 minutes per mile. In fact, that is what I did for 40+ miles.
I felt great, strong and hydrated. Everything was working well,

all systems go. Zero issues. I used salt capsules and plenty of ice to cool my core, which was key to getting me to where I was in the race.

The trails were not too grueling, and everything is runnable. There are rocky technical areas that were tricky in the dark with tired eyes and tired feet. All the hills were not too bad. The terrain is desert dirt! I ran in Nike Free 5.0s which are street shoes. I feel like I was fine with these; something heavier would have slowed me down. I had no plans for a pacer, or a crew. I did send out a few messages to see if anyone wanted to stop by the race, and my buddy Cliff and his sister Carrie came by! It was starting to get really hot, and this was a nice boost to see them. I really appreciated them coming, but right after I saw them, I started having awful stomach cramps. And at the same time, the heat of the day started to get to me. I had ice in a buff that I kept putting on my face, neck, and body, ice under my hat, and all of my heat gear on. My core just started to get too hot, and my stomach cramps were wearing me down. I knew I couldn't run through it. When I ran, it hurt more. Soooooo, I walked...

I walked 10 miles to Jackass Junction. I just kept moving forward. I was using less energy and was not as hot anymore. I had to be smart and listen to my body, not my brain. My brain said run through it; my body said walk you Jackass! I had to improvise. Plan A was not going to work anymore. My Ace of Spades up my sleeve apparently was having the mental capacity and ability to power walk, and for a looooong time. At this point,

252

I had met up with Tonja. She is someone I actually interviewed with about a job--small world! She said that I needed to work on my breathing and work the acid out. So that's exactly what I did. I ended up walking mostly from Jackass back to Jeadquarters working on belly breathing. Then around 5:00, the angry sun was going down behind the mountains, and it was time to run again!!! Thanks again Tonja!

Another thing a lot of veterans said was to make sure to eat. I ate plenty of watermelon and used Tailwind as part of my nutrition. I had to start putting something more solid into my system because I was getting low on energy. They had a large variety of food and snacks at the aid stations, but nothing sounded appealing. I had to

253

eat, or I was screwed. They had Ramen noodles in vegetable broth, so I figured it was safe. It surely was; I ate the shit out of it for the remainder of the race! With the sun gone, I felt much better. My stomach was fine. No muscle pain at all--truly amazing, as I had surpassed 60 miles (Now in uncharted waters, personal best for distance). I ran on and off when I could and started resting for a few minutes at the aid stations while I had my soup, which gave my feet a well-deserved rest. I started to have low energy again, so I tapped in to caffeinated Tailwind. Nothing. No lift.

Life had to go on. I didn't feel like running, but knew I needed to keep moving forward. Soooooo, back to the Ace of Spades, more power walking. I knew I would finish but knew it would be taking me much longer than projected. I probably power walked 30 of the last 40 miles! I could walk faster than I could run! The problem was that it was a long time between aid stations. They seem to never be getting closer. Each time I arrived, it was a boost--more soup and another milestone closer to finishing this thing.

During the course of the race, I saw one runner black out while running, others unconscious at aid stations, and many with severe cramping. The temperature reaches 102 degrees during the day. It was not Badwater, but it was no joke either. Badwater 135 is the ultramarathon race in Death Valley, the lowest point in the U.S. with the highest temperatures. 250 of the 100-mile runners did not finish. Runners who did not protect themselves from the elements simply did not make it. One idiot was boasting and bragging at the aid station that he had already drunk 22 beers and was planning on drinking 50 beers during the race. He did not make it.

I got to see the sunrise for the second time during the race on mile 92. The end was near, but I was not there yet!

Hallucination, I think not.

There it was. I could hear the music too, Jeadquarters and the finish line! 25 hours, 17 minutes and 6 seconds later, my first 100 miler is in the books. I felt GREAT! Mentally exhausted, physically fine, just some tired feet! I saw some spiders, a rattlesnake that I lost sight of, some little badger things that may have been cute Gremlins, and heard a lot of coyotes howling when the sun went down. I only saw one, who was friendly and probably would make a great pet.

I would not call it hallucinations like something you might see on 'shrooms or acid, but Holy shit, everything is so freaking trippy, especially at night. Everything looks like Willy Wonka or Super Mario Brothers. When my flashlight or headlight came across some of the cactus, bushes, and other things I stopped a bunch of times just to make sure of what the hell I was actually looking at! Two different times I heard runners mention the full moon. There was no full moon; it was the globe domed lights as you were approaching Headquarters. It was funny to see some of the costumes at night; I was trying to figure what the fuck was coming towards me! At least during the night, it was hard to see men who obviously were trying to win The Best Ass contest. I got stuck behind some G-string fool for waaaaaay too long during the day. Glad he didn't stop short.

So again, this was an absolutely amazing experience; I would do it again in a heartbeat. 100 miles is a long time to run, walk, or just be in my own head. I took 194,850 steps. That's a lot of steps. It literally is like running from Waltham, Massachusetts to

Dennis, Massachusetts, Waltham to Portland, Maine, and from Waltham to and past Hartford, CT!

People cannot understand why I or someone would want to do this. I feel we all owe it to ourselves to see what our own bodies are capable of. Life is too short to sit back and not do crazy shit.

I love this quote by Henry Rollins: "In the winter I plot and plan, in spring I move." I ran a few of the RAW series 5ks in the fall and had 2017 pretty much all planned out.

In winter, I plot and plan. In spring, I move.
Henry Rollins

Chapter 42

National Personal Training Institute Waltham, Massachusetts October 3, 2016

"You can't be afraid to make major life decisions"

I always say you can't be afraid to make major life decisions. living at my parents' house still was not a deal. But I knew it wasn't forever. Both myself and Alejandra were still unemployed, and I had the opportunity to do something I always wanted to do. I was still completely burned out from the food industry and I always wanted to go to personal training school or do something related to exercise and running. There was a personal training school 3 1/2 miles away from my parents and there was a 6-month course full-time. People including family members questioned not only my running, my traveling, which was already paid for and my decision to enroll in the school. I was sick and tired of doing what I was doing and was trying to transition out of it. As I mentioned before I'm an opportunist; an opportunity came up and when would I ever have the chance to go to school again while not working? It was only six months and time goes by fast--especially when you're busy. So, between taking care of my family, running, going to school and studying and then having a few races on the schedule, time sure did go by fast. I really, really enjoyed this program and learned a lot from it. I say you can always make more money, but you can't get back time. It seems like this was the right time to do this and I believe it was. I went with my intuition, again.

Between exercising in class, exercising on my own and with all the running I was doing, I was the most fit that I've ever been. My first

260

day of class was the day after the Maine Marathon. I was hesitant to take time off, but I already registered for Javelina Jundred, which was week 4 at my school. I was allowed to make up the work and didn't skip a beat. The month leading up to Javelina I focused more on the weights and getting stronger which in turn helped me during the race. Also, I was quickly learning more and more about my own body and how to assess things so I could readjust if needed. As time went by, while I was in school, I started thinking about employment. I also started thinking about where we wanted to or where we could live. It started to become stressful as the months went on. It was tight in my parents' house and we had several conversations about living there. We had already surpassed the amount of time that we agreed to live there. Life happened and kept happening and then I enrolled in school so we decided that May of 2017 would be our deadline to move out.

In February we started seeing family counseling. This was a good opportunity to have a neutral party to give us unbiased advice--and quite frankly, to figure out where we can live. The first appointment was a consultation and we talked about what we wanted to achieve as a couple. At the second appointment the counselor asked me what was bothering me, and what I wanted to talk about. And I said I wanted to talk about where we were going to live. I was going to graduate on April 2nd. I needed to start applying for work. I needed to know where to apply, which state we had talked about possibly moving to—to Florida, to New York, to Colorado, somewhere in Massachusetts, New Hampshire, and Arizona. I wasn't about to just start applying around the country for jobs. I kind of wanted to narrow it down to one or two states or to make a decision.

261

What if I got a job in another state, are we prepared to move? We both knew that once we moved from Chelmsford if we wanted to live in Massachusetts we would have to live <u>farther</u> away and being <u>farther</u> away we weren't happy—we weren't even happy in Chelmsford because that was too far. But in order to afford anything that we wanted we would have to do that, and we weren't willing to. Move to New Hampshire? That's even farther away! And then we started saying that we didn't want to live anywhere that had a long cold winter so that pretty much ruled out New York. Colorado? Cross those off the list. The woman said, "Where would you live if you could live anywhere?" And I said, "Arizona." "Arizona?" "Yes Arizona." She then asked Alejandra, "Where would you like to live, did you hear what Henry is saying?" Alejandra said she could live in Arizona. What the hell, it took two counseling visits to figure out where to live! Why couldn't we just talk about this on our own! Regardless, we literally shook hands, laughed and said, "We had a deal." Then we started taking steps towards moving, tying up loose ends and making plans. Another major life decision.

Chapter 43

12 hour Treadmillathon Corning, NY 2-19-17

Our great friends Enrique and Maritza were gracious enough to post my second fundraising event for Runwell. It's the way my running career started, and if it wasn't for them who knows, maybe I never would have even started running. They own a Snap Fitness 24-hour gym on Market Street in downtown Corning, New York. This would be the location for the 12 hour treadmillathon. The day before, we had a TV interview, a radio interview and then another interview the morning of, and then one during the actual treadmillathon. It is pretty cool walking around town because people knew Enrique; then they saw me and said, "Hey, you're the guy that's going to do that 12-hour treadmill run." It was like we were both celebrities. Pretty neat!

I ran the first 50 miles in my Luna sandals and then ended up finishing with 78 total miles in 12 hours. It wasn't about the number of miles; it was about the time there and the impact I made. A lot of people came up to me while I was running or walking on the treadmill and wanted to hear my story about my recovery, and some people actually ran or walked beside me. One guy that never ran more than three miles ended up running / walking over 13 miles. Another person that had never run more than 2 or 3 miles ran five and somebody else that never walked more than three miles walked 7 miles. It was not necessarily all about recovery but also ended up being about motivating people too. And just like running with a friend or in a group when you share the miles, they go by a lot quicker. Those people didn't even realize how far they had gone until they stopped and checked. It was pretty cool to see people go past their perceived limits and barriers. I raised over $2,000 and this event set me up for bigger things down the road such as the Boston Marathon Quads. Being on a treadmill for 12 hours is no joke; you really have to stay present. You have to go to a special place in your mind and just convince yourself that this is what you are going to do and just keep doing it and doing it and doing it and doing it and doing it.

Badwater Cape Fear 51 Miler 3-18-17

This was another runcation that had been on my bucket list for 2 years and honestly was one of my favorite races of all times. Badwater events attract very good quality people and it's like family. I was immediately accepted. David Clark was there again, and I met Charlie Engle for the first time. In fact, I hung out with both of them at the expo and then ran the first 15 miles side by side with Charlie. We talked about sobriety, recovery and pain management. You start basically running roads for the first eight miles and then a mile through some trails that are like a jungle. Then you go down a sandy ramp onto the beach, and you actually run on the beach up to Fisher point. You come back to the start, and then run back out to Fisher Point again, and then finish. It was super windy. If you are a slower runner, the tide was coming in by 10 AM and you would not have too much quality sand to run on. I started out with Charlie and we were moving at a good clip. We get out to Fisher Point in no time, so we had plenty of good beach sand to run on and even when we turned around on the way back, but the tide was rapidly coming in. It started to get very sloped. If you want good sand to run on, you have to run right next to the water and then kind of dodge the waves. So that's what I did. Going out to Fisher Point and coming back I was in third place. Then as I headed out again I was feeling strong, but I was three miles from there and started to bonk a little bit, and my pace diminished. I need nutrition. Bonking means you have depleted your glycogen stores. You have a calorie deficit and hit the wall. You need to eat before that happens. For the first time ever, my body started craving real food during an ultra.

265

When I got to Fisher Point, I made myself two plates of food and literally sat there for like 7 to 10 minutes to properly eat. Twenty runners passed me between bonking and eating; I knew that was okay. I knew that I had fuel which meant I could catch a lot of them. I couldn't catch all of them and ended up finishing in 10th place, but that was ahead of a lot of strong runners. I pushed as hard as hard as I possibly could the whole race. I finished 51 miles in under 8 hours. This reassured me that all the resistance training in and outside of school really, really helped me during this race and I felt like I was the strongest I've ever been. I learned more about fueling and more about running through fatigue and pain.

Myself, my great mentors David Clark and Charlie Engle

Chapter 44
<u>Boston Marathon Quad April 1st, 2017</u>

This was my third major fundraising concept for Runwell, on the road to Patagonia 2017. The Boston Marathon Quad is the Boston Marathon course four consecutive times. This is the progression to doing the marathon course twice like I had done the previous year. I literally just finished personal training school two days before, and carefully watched the weather take a turn for the worse. I had not yet qualified for the actual 2017 Boston Marathon (I qualified for 2018 for the Maine Marathon) which was scheduled for three weeks down the road, and I didn't want to interfere with the actual marathon or run anywhere close to it, so I decided to just pick this date and then start promoting it. Little did I know that the weather turned from possible rain, to freezing rain, to Nor'easter over the course of a few days. The morning of the Quad, I remember Alejandra coming out of the shower. As she was getting dressed, I told her it was snowing, and she didn't believe me. The windows are all fogged up inside the house and she did not have her glasses on. When she put her glasses on and we cleared the window she couldn't believe it. Snow. Well, the snow proved to be the least of my problems as the freezing rain and running in a foot of slush ended up putting people in the hospital.

On another note, I came up with a spreadsheet where runners can put their names during certain time slots so I could see who I might be picking up to join me along the way, and so that other runners could possibly share rides or go out and back together. This proved to be very helpful for everybody involved. What happened was really cool. People met other people for the first time, including myself meeting some people for the first time, and others made friends for life…pretty cool. I had several TV interviews leading up to this and others were supposed to cover my journey along the route, but the weather was so bad that they just didn't make it out or they couldn't find us. It started out with a small group from the finish line on Boylston Street and we started making our way towards Hopkinton. We ran through Coolidge Corner and then on to the hills of Newton. This was no joke going backwards. Without inclement weather it was hard enough, and now I get freezing, driving rain, snow and ice in the face. We were running literally in a foot of slushy water at times in the carriage road while getting splashed by cars. Good times! And all I had was 9,697 miles to go! What we didn't know was that this would not let up. I had a couple of really strong runners with me and they had to drop out because of potential hypothermia, not being able to get warm with uncontrolled shivering. We went into every Dunkin Donuts that we saw. That was our savior. At a minimum, we would use the hand dryers to attempt to dry out our gloves and hats somewhat; they were completely soaked. Caffeine and croissants definitely helped too, but those hand dryers saved us.

We had to keep moving forward, we picked up runners along the way and finally made it to Hopkinton. Once we arrived at the starting line there, I wanted to do a Facebook live thing. I could not even get my gloves off. They were so wet, and my hands were so cold that I couldn't even operate my phone. The freezing rain kept hitting my phone and would not allow me to use the touch screen. Oh my God, my crippled fingers were not able to function either. I could not use my phone. I even had to have help getting my wet gloves back on my hands. I needed help getting my phone in my pocket. I had four layers on top including a waterproof and a windproof jacket, three layers on my legs, socks and running shoes, plus gloves. When we got to one of the Dunkin Donuts, I called my wife to grab my heavy-duty Gore-Tex pants and meet me at the fire station, where I had a room I was allowed to use as my major aid station in Newton. We picked up more runners along the way and everybody suffered together. The weather warmed up a little bit, so it turned into snow which was much better, but we were still running in slushy conditions. I had zero blisters on my feet despite being completely waterlogged the whole time and cold. My feet were killing me from the pain of pounding on the cement. We made it to the finish line; two marathons in the books.

Running on One Foot?

It was dark for a while and we had a long, cold death march to the start line. We stopped at the fire station again and regrouped, and I remember changing my socks and shoes and putting my feet up for a little bit and then I had new life. Once we started again something was wrong, I couldn't run. I ended up doing a walk/ run ratio, but I couldn't put any pressure on my right foot. We kept moving until we came to a Dunkin Donuts to assess what was going on with my foot. I massaged it, I looked at it, I poked it, and nothing hurt to the touch but every time I ran it felt like it was broken. I never felt anything like this before so with this unknown pain and injury I wondered what to do. All I could think of was that we were going to Mexico the following day and what would happen if I broke my foot? It's kind of weird because when I walked on it, it didn't hurt but as soon as I started running, it would feel like it was going to explode. I was tired but knew I could push through. I have been through worse, but this was different. I had no idea what was wrong with my foot, I honestly assumed it was broken, if not shattered. We did a walk/run ratio, mostly walk. We ran when we felt cold, we ran to get warm. Once we were getting close to Hopkinton, I made a decision to call it. I had nothing to prove as I had raised about $2,500 and created a lot of dialogue about addiction and recovery with the media, on Facebook and with all the people that shared my life changing journey with me the past 24 hours. I come to find out there were a bunch of people that opened up to me about their struggles with addiction during our run; I had no idea. Never suffer in silence' tell someone you are struggling, that you need help, anyone. Admitting you have a problem is the first step.

I had nothing to prove. I needed to save something to run for another day. I got a ride home, got a little bit of rest and went to the hospital in the morning. At this point my ankle was swollen up to a cankle and the doctors and nurses (all seven of them in the room) were pointing and talking about my foot and they diagnosed it with "overuse." Nothing was really wrong; there was just a bunch of fluid that was protecting my potentially damaged ankle. "RICE" is what was prescribed for my recovery. RICE is an acronym for Rest, Ice, Compression, Elevation. At least it wasn't broken, and we were on our way to Mexico later that day.

Written CBS Boston: Boston Marathon Quad April 2017

270

http://boston.eicbslocal.com/2017/03/26/addicts-treatment-ultra-runner-henry-ward-boston-marathon-walt meham/

Video CBS Boston: Boston Marathon Quad April 2017
http://boston.cbslocal.com/2017/03/26/addicts-treatment-ultra-runner-henry-ward-boston-marathon-waltham/

Chapter 45
<u>24 Hour Track Run, Belmont, MA 4-25-17</u>

After the swelling in my feet went down, yes both feet swelled up in Mexico. I did a little bit of running down there to recover and do a little touristy thing on foot and then I started thinking about "what's next." I asked Alejandra if I could do one more event before we moved to Arizona, kind of one last hurrah, one more fundraising concept. "When is enough, enough?" I wanted to do a 24-hour track run with Becca Pizzi and the Belmont Track Club. There were so many runners that couldn't find us or did not come out because of the weather for the Boston Marathon Quad. With some significant convincing, she said okay. The general concept was to start at 6:00 am on Monday morning and then run the first 23 hours, and then the last hour I would finish up Tuesday morning with the track group.

I pulled up and grabbed my bags of gear, water and nutrition and walked towards the track to put everything down on the bench. I looked over and there's a camera guy with lights and scaffolding up in the bleachers. He came over and asked if I was Henry Ward. He was from one CBS Boston news station and wanted to know if he could do a story, so I obliged. I got to share my story about recovery and why I want to do this fundraising event. Shortly after he left another news team came and wanted to do a story and then my friends started showing up. After that, the most exciting thing that happened for a few hours occurred when one of the maintenance guys from the high school came out of the garage with

272

a John Deere tractor and I watched him cut the grass of the softball and baseball fields.

Adrenaline Carried Me; The Media Carried My Message
Over the course of the day and the night, lots of people came. We shared many laughs, we ran or walked laps as we often talked about all things addiction and struggles. The weather was sunny during the day and cool during the night. It was pretty neat seeing a car pull up behind the other cars on Concord Street, because I knew it was going to be a runner; I just was not sure who. I wasn't sure until they actually walked onto the track and it was always great to see somebody new, somebody else to keep me going. There was a lot of walking overnight, two laps run, two laps walk, something like that and I had a considerable amount of pain in my feet and one of my knees. One of my friends Scot, who ran track showed up at 4:00 AM. And at that point I could barely run because I was in so much pain. I said I'm feeling really disappointed as I knew there would be media there in the morning and all my Belmont Track friends are going to show up for the on-hour track run that we did every Tuesday morning. I felt that if I did too much earlier, I would be letting them down because I would not be able to run. It was a crazy phenomenon. The media showed up again and there were literally five different vehicles waiting for the final hour and waiting to interview me after the actual event finished. Once they started showing up my friends started showing up. I can't explain it, but all of a sudden, I was running again and pain-free. I think I was full of adrenaline and the blood was rushing through my body and my veins enough to drown out any pain I was feeling for the previous couple hours. I actually ran the track workout. I did three

273

interviews afterwards and they took some additional video and still shots of myself and my group. I raised another $2,500 from this event for Runwell. This was another successful event. At this point I'm really grateful for running because it gave me this platform; it gave me a larger stage. I'm grateful for the media assistance in getting my message out there, as well.

CBS Boston: 24 hour track run May 2017
http://boston.cbslocal.com/2017/04/24/henry-ward-belmont-track-running-24-hours-addiction-charity/

ABC Boston: 24 hour track run May 2017
http://www.wcvb.com/article/man-runs-24-hours-to-raise-addiction-treatment-awareness/9557455

Belmont Patch article: 24 hour track run May 2017
https://patch.com/massachusetts/belmont/ultra-marathoner-recovering-addict-runs-24-hours-belmont-high-track

Chapter 46

Moving to Arizona/Breaking My Foot June, 2017

I had already gone out to Arizona and enrolled Sebastian into kindergarten, secured an apartment and had a new job as a hands-on chef. I flew out and worked a few weeks, then went back to tie up a few loose ends and it was almost time to finish packing, see the movers off and drive cross-country with Alejandra and Sebastian. We decided to wait until Sebastian finished Pre-K. My sister Amy invited the family over for a cookout to celebrate my niece Jadyn's birthday. It happened to be Father's Day, our anniversary. It was also kind of a going away party for us. I had a really, really good time but it was kind of sad seeing the kids play for the last time for a while and I had fun playing with them, too. We said goodbye 20 times and it was dark in the front yard. I was playing soccer with the kids, I let them keep the soccer ball away from me and they were falling down laughing hysterically. It was so much fun to see. Then I grabbed the ball and started fooling around and juking left and right and kind of goofing around. Then I came off the ball with my right leg and rolled my ankle really hard. There was a snap, crackle, and pop. Of course, the week previously I made the mistake of saying I've never broken a bone in my life. I had a feeling it was broken. It swelled up right away and I usually don't swell. We went in the house and decided it was best to go to the hospital to get X-rays. Sure enough, I broke my fibula along with a severely sprained ankle. Pretty ironic—I break my leg while fooling around, but not with all the running I was doing! Sebastian's graduation was later that week and then two days later we were to drive cross-country. I went to see an orthopedic doctor in the

275

middle of the week and it just so happened to be the Boston Celtics' orthopedist. I told him about my running, and he said, "I suppose you want the answer to the million-dollar question." "So, you should be able to run probably in 3 to 5 weeks. You'll know when you're able to jump up and down on one foot and land on it pain free." He said, "I don't suggest doing it today, tomorrow or the next day or next week; be patient and try in about three weeks and see how you feel. He asked if I wanted to go to PT and I told him I just completed personal training school and I can probably just do it myself if he gave me the exercises. He told me to ditch the crutches and work on mobility. Which is exactly what I did a couple of times a day along with the pool and calf raises and circular motions, followed by very gentle kicking motions.

At this point I had to start working. I was working 10 to 12 hours a day on my feet. After the first week I was concerned the swelling wouldn't go down but once my ankle responded well to the mobility work I was doing, miraculously the swelling started to go down and the pain subsided. After 3 weeks I did a couple of gentle jumps. I could feel the pain a little bit. The following day I started hiking and did some very light jogging. I incorporated some elliptical work and rode the gym bike at our apartment to keep my conditioning up. I did body weight exercises. As I lay there on the ground at my sister's house, all I could think about was that it was broken. I thought for sure Patagonia was in jeopardy because that was only 4 months away. But once I learned it was a non-weight-bearing bone and I had time to recover, I felt a lot better about life in general. I continued to do the mobility work, strength and conditioning faithfully to get it back to normal as quickly as possible. I started

276

showing up for group runs and I always finished DFL. (Dead F*c#@ng last.) I was able to run at least, it was getting better and if I didn't hurt anymore Patagonia was going to happen. Once the swelling went down and I had no pain I decided to do a 24-hour desert run in the middle of August as a fundraising concept for Runwell.

24 Hour Desert Run 8/15/17

I was very busy working 50 to 60 hours a week at a minimum. Work was very demanding, and management required chefs to work a minimum of 10 hours a day, and 10 hours was never enough for them. I got to cross train at work, which was good and bad. Bad because I was recovering from a broken foot, good because I was getting paid to lift things! Time was an issue, so I got to work out at work. I was pushing and pulling and lifting at work and putting in 30,000 steps a day. Also, it was 110 degrees in the kitchen at times, literally. The air conditioning was broken for a month in the summer! Heat training! I got great training and preparation for a 24-hour desert run in the middle of the summer in the middle of the desert where I was thinking about doing it.

I wanted to meet some new friends and do at least one more fundraiser for Patagonia which was approaching rapidly. So, I decided to organize a 24-Hour Desert Run, and basically run around Tempe Town Lake. We ventured off to Papago Park, the splash pad at Tempe Marketplace and played around in fountains in an office park. Just like the other events I did, people shared with me their struggles. We ran and chatted, and we talked a lot about addiction

277

as we passed hundreds of homeless people, who do not want to be the way they are as we ran around Tempe Town Lake. We agreed that most men don't want to be the way they are, just like addicts and alcoholics. We shared a lot of laughs and I met some friends for life. A couple of people I was already friends with, including Ed Gildersleeve and Lisa Buzzeo, who both met me at the start and ended up logging over 30 miles with me. I met a lot of new friends that I still run with today. It was well over 100 degrees and I suffered. The running community here helped me get the entire 24-hour run done. They helped remind me who I was, what I stood for, and helped me find a way to finish this sufferfest. The Lord knows that I suffered a lot more during my active addiction years and this was nothing. This was another life changing experience. I raised $1,500 for this event. With that, I started making an impact on the Arizona community. I had intentions of doing more fundraising events for Patagonia; this would be the last one. I continued to train well, running with my pack often with 15 and 20 lbs in it-- sometimes more because that's what I would be doing in Patagonia.

Chapter 47
The Road to Patagonia/Almost There!

There was a mandatory list of gear we needed to bring--at least 14,000 calories of food and nutrition, all of which you had to carry. If you wanted to bring seven pairs of underwear you had to carry that. If you wanted to bring three jackets you had to carry them. You had to carry the mandatory list of gear; anything else you wanted to bring you had to take it with you. Nothing would be transported for you. Included in those items was a sleeping bag, air mattress. The only thing that Racing the Planet supplied was water in the tent, and hot water for cooking your meals. So basically, my pack weighed 25 pounds when I checked my gear in, and I would need to run with it. You cannot just put a 25 lb pack on and start running and expect to do well--and more importantly, expect not to get injured, because you will get injured. Running with a heavy pack takes practice. Your hips do not swivel as much, and obviously it puts a little more burden on your legs and your glutes. I gradually increased the weight and increased the miles to prevent injury. I was pretty comfortable running with 20 lbs. I often trained with a watermelon inside my pack or a bunch of water bottles. I had gone through my gear a hundred times and gotten some solid advice, especially from Linda Quirk who had done a bunch of these stage races before. I eliminated half of the extra stuff that I wanted to bring, such as the seven pairs of underwear! I ended up raising over $12,000 for Runwell as part of my "Road to Patagonia" campaign.

It was an honor and a privilege to be able to take part in this race. I am forever grateful for all the donations and for the guidance from Runwell (Linda Quirk and Kim Pawelek) and from coach Lisa Smith-Batchen. Thanks to my super awesome wife Alejandra Hernandez for putting up with me and my training and allowing me to do this. Thanks to my great Runwell teammates Ashley and Brian Carr; we are now friends for life. 4 Deserts and Racing the Planet put on a well-organized event. Everything was top notch, from the organizers to the volunteers, the doctors, and the local staff.

Basically, all we did was run, recover, eat, camp and hang out for 7 days, and take care of our bodies. There are a few details in between which I will try and get into here and describe the best I can what transpired in Patagonia. The first 4 stages were slated for 25 miles each stage, the long march was 50 miles, and the final stage was to be 4 miles. I lived off of Generation Ucan Bars and coffee for breakfast, Ramen noodles for lunch and dinner, Swell Balls as fuel while running, and had a bunch of snacks for treats when needed, including a freeze-dried ice cream sandwich, Starbursts. I had 3 camp meals that I ate when I was super hungry. I used 99% of my mandatory gear and alllll my clothes. I am happy with my gear selections. I needed to have gear and clothing that was practical, light, and did not take up space! My training and nutrition were spot on. I would not change a thing for next time. Maybe I would have done just a little more steep climbing, though I did a lot.

I arrived after traveling for 37 hours. I assume this was mental training for what was in store for me! It was great to be there even

280

though I was brain dead tired. I got checked in and slept well. The next morning, we had breakfast and a briefing, and after that was our mandatory equipment check-in. I had everything but was unsure about it, being my first time doing one of these races. I was good to go; I just needed to figure out how to get everything into my backpack. We needed to carry all mandatory equipment and 14,000 calories minimum for the week in our packs. Any items that you did not bring, you would be penalized or not allowed to run. Anything more than that, you carry more weight! With my pack around 25 pounds, Yikes! That is 1/6 of my body weight. I had to run 155 miles with this thing attached to my shoulders and back! I certainly put the time in running with the pack and there was no turning back now. After that we all got in the vehicles and were driven to camp.

We arrived and quickly discovered that the athletes who were there already were putting on life jackets and were getting into rafts. We had to cross rapids to get to camp! It was off to an adventurous start! We arrived and a lot of people were a bundle of nerves including me. Not about running but how the hell I was going to fit everything into my backpack! We ate and hung out during the day and night and met some really cool people. We were all in this thing together. I got some broken sleep and then it was time to get up and pee, eat, and get ready for day one of running and day one of shoving everything in the backpack. Thank God for Ashley Carr. She was my awesome teammate and the voice of reason who helped keep me calm and get everything into my backpack! We had a race briefing at 7:30 AM and were told that we would be running up a dirt road, then scrambling up a hill where we would see some beautiful rock formations. That would be 23 miles total. That was

281

true but before we scrambled, we completed a relentless climb! The views were stunning and well worth the work. As we made our way down fighting through rough brush, I saw wild horses running freely. We hopped on to a dirt path and I saw an armadillo for the first time ever. This really made me feel happy and propelled me towards the finish line of day 1.

Back to camp to recuperate by stretching, eating and hanging out with athletes in the cold river. Then it was eat again, stretch, hang out by the fire until bedtime. I slept well but it was really cold at night. The next morning it was pretty much the same deal; get up and get ready for stage 2. We were told that it was going to be shorter than stage 1, and flatter. This was true, but not true! There were certainly some hills and we ran 18 miles. What's the difference between 23 and 19? Not much! We crossed pampas and forests and yeah, it was a little less grueling than stage 1. I felt great during this stage and finished with some confirmation that I have got this. The pack was slightly lighter each day as we were eating some of its contents.

The next 2 stages are kind of a blur. I do recall that the weather started to change as we experienced the winds of Patagonia throughout the day and while at camp. I had significant wind burn on my face and lips to the point of them bleeding on and off for 5 days. The rains chilled me to the bone as well. Nothing really I haven't run in before, but had not done in a long time as we moved to the desert! Sleeping in the cold was not ideal, but there were no other options for accommodations

"What kept me going? I knew there were 25 million Americans out there suffering more than I was from addiction…I am recovering. I can do anything."

Fast forward to stage 5, the long march. This was slated for 55 miles, but due to the rain causing the snow on the mountains to melt, it was reduced to 46 miles. The rivers that we were supposed to cross became too deep and fast and were impassable. I saved something in the tank for this one. At least I thought I did! We had to climb over 6000 meters on this day, and a significant part of the climbing came early. It was raining, cold and windy which turned dirt into mud! It was slippery as well. The rivers we crossed were frigid, and a few were rapid and up to the bottom of my shorts. I thought the climbing would never end. When the initial climb was over, I had tired legs, and could barely pick up my feet. I must have kicked every tree, root and rock, and fell 5 times. My feet were destroyed at this point and I was in a considerable amount of pain. The 2 things I really needed to get me to the finish line were very angry at me (yes, my feet!). Negativity set in, and I was miserable. I wanted this to be over, and my thoughts of finishing this stage in fewer than 12 hours in the daylight seemed bleak at best. The only 2 things that kept me going were that I knew there were 25 million Americans out there suffering more than I was from addiction, and that 9 years ago to the day I was too weak to go to the liquor store for more booze, too weak to shower, and thought I was dying from alcohol. I was dying, I wanted to die. I had little fight left in me. It was the last day I ever touched alcohol. I got through that day, I am recovering from addiction, I can do anything. On this long march day, I was stronger than I was that day, much stronger. I could get through this. I just wasn't sure how. The fight was on. It was the

283

single most challenging runs for me, but I was not going to give up. I was going to finish this and finish strong.

"The pain was not going away, but I was no longer dwelling on it."

I finally arrived at an aid station and rumor had it that there was hot chocolate! That put a huge smile on my face. In fact, this was the game changer; this was what I needed to get me out of my own head. It changed my mood and changed my day. ALL OF A SUDDEN, I AM NOW ABLE TO RUN AGAIN, AND RUN HARD! This hot chocolate was a gift from God. It was not the caffeine, it was not the warmth, it was simply something that helped me forget the misery. My feet still hurt, and I knew the pain was not going away, but I was no longer dwelling on it. There were more hills and more rivers, but for the most part it was full speed ahead. The driving rain and wind was still there, my face was still bleeding but the finish line was drawing nearer. I saw Ashley Carr, my awesome teammate at the next aid station which was also a huge boost. We discovered we had less than 20k left and that meant finishing well before darkness. I now had even more bounce in my step. Ashley and I more or less ran together for the rest of this stage. In fact, we would finish together. This was an amazing day that I will never forget. I thought I was done; I thought at a minimum I would finish around 20 hours and ended up finishing 11 hours 8 minutes. I was frozen, confused as to what transpired but knew it was over. Thank you Ashley for helping me.

The next morning, I wound up in the medical tent with hypothermia. I could not get warm. Everything happens for a reason. I was there to witness Michelle finish her day/night somewhere around the 26-hour mark. She walked through the night as the rivers rose, the winds got stronger, and the temps dropped. She was frozen but overcome with gratitude and a sense of self accomplishment. I gave her my blanket. She told me she was a breast cancer survivor and if she could conquer that, she could do anything. I was so happy for her. I shared my story with her--the abridged version. I told her I was super proud of her for finding a way to get it done. She is a warrior.

I found my way to the medical tent again, this time to have my feet taken care of again. I had been doing so myself, this time I needed help. I had stubbed my toes one too many times and had blisters under the nails. The doctor had to drill 4 nails to get the fluid out in order to relieve the pressure. To say the least, it was difficult to walk. The sun came out, and it was a day of resting by the fire and drying out everything I had. Everything was soaked from the long march. We did not have to run today, and tomorrow was only 4 miles.

On Saturday morning we were told we would start running at 5:30AM. We were up and ready. Just 4 miles to the finish line and that was it. I decided that I would savor the last miles, the last moments and recollect this past week. What an incredible week it was. It was challenging, peaceful, fun, and beautiful. I thought of all those who made donations, I thought of how much has changed since I registered for this race in March of 2016. I thought of my

285

broken fibula in June, and how lucky I was to still be able to recover from that and be in the race. As I approached the finish line, I heard there was pizza and empanadas, so I sprinted to the end. I must have had 10 of each! We took some photos by the glacier at the end and enjoyed the food and drinks. Then we took a 2-hour bus ride back to the hotel.

It was over, but well worth all the training, planning, fundraising. We crossed over 30 rivers, there were 50 countries representing over 300 athletes. I met some of the most amazing athlete, and humans.

It took 32 hours to travel back and I went back to work the next day. My feet ballooned up and I spent the next 3 days dealing with and taking care of them. The show must go on at work. We needed to prepare 4,000 turkey dinners! I would rest over the weekend and start training for Coldwater Rumble 100 miler in January. It is only 20 miles away. At least there will not be any ultratraveling!

25 pounds to be carried by me.

The usual suspects.

Ashley and Brian Carr, my awesome teammates.

Glorious trails I will never
forget.

Women's winner Sarah Sawyer approaching a cow that was on the trail!

Brian Carr enjoying a hot beverage.

Bloodied from the wind and rain, I bled for 5 days on and off...

Me, Ashley, Peter, Brian. Tentmates!

Allllll done, I was destroyed. This was pre hot chocolate. I was hurting like I never had before.

Typical climb.

Mas Gauchos!

Cold and wet, still

Camping was epic!

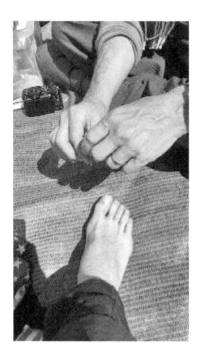

**I had 4 toenails drilled to relieve
pressure.**

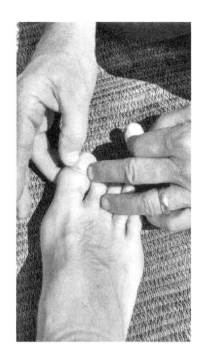

SMH.

Me, Nicole and Michelle!

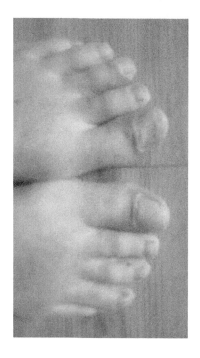

Need new feet..

Glacier at the finish.

My feet blew up at LAX. Sneakers would not
fit.

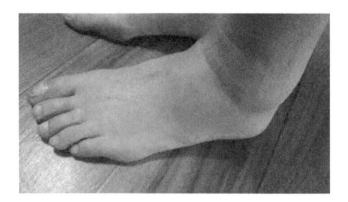

Yikes. Flashbacks to Boston Quad!

Recovery hike with Seabass!!!!

Chapter 48
Boston Marathon Quad 4-15-18

So, let me start off by saying the Boston quad which is the Boston Marathon course 4 consecutive times was one of the best things I have ever experienced. The weather was horrendous. It started off with snow, then freezing rain, hail, then downpours. I have accepted that inclement weather seems to follow me.

I was picked-up by Scot and Amy Dedeo, and we got dropped off in Boston 1.5 miles from the finish line, our starting line. We were not going to make it in time, so Scot and I ran! We met up with Sean Butler and Rich Morrissey, took a few pictures then stopped in Adidas runbase to say a quick hello to Anne Margaret! Then, we were off and on our way to Hopkinton! I was surprised to see another friend, a non-runner who was on a mountain bike. He came out to the course to see us and see if we needed anything. He said he was going to go 1 mile up and then one mile back. His name is Sean Fraser. He ended up biking in the snow alongside Sean Butler all the way to Hopkinton! He said he has only ridden a bike for about 2 miles in the past 20 years!

It gets a little blurry but Scot, Rich, and I made our way towards Hopkinton and met up with Eric and Mindy. Mindy was running the next day, so she drove up to meet up at the starting line and Eric ran with us. We get to the starting line and meet Mindy. Thanks for the Ucan bar Mindy! I was pretty cold because I was so wet for so long. I was expecting to see Lisa and Brian. I had them on the spreadsheet for picking me up and taking me from Hopkinton

304

towards Boston. I spent 20 minutes looking for them around the common. I was freezing, and I said, "Oh man, they blew me off."

As I started to run, I remembered that I probably didn't delete them from the spreadsheet that I copied and pasted from last year—my bad!!! So, there I was running by myself in the dark, snow and the freezing rain heading towards Boston. Negativity started to creep in, and I had to quickly quiet the voices in my head. Otherwise, I knew I would be done. I started running fairly hard to keep warm and I got to the Dunkin Donuts and dried off in the hair dryer a little bit. At least I dried my hat and my gloves. Around mile 10 of the marathon route, I saw Roger and Mary Wright! They pulled up in a car and said they were going to meet me at the 13-mile mark. A big boost—someone to run with and one of my favorite people, to boot! Roger gave me a chocolate chip chia, something that was pretty tasty. Onwards towards the fire station we went. It gets even blurrier, but I met up with Peter Guza and then some of the Waltham wussies like Tommy, Cara Stephanie, Jack, Manny, eventually Randy, and Tim. I don't remember if it was going out or coming back but they ran with me for about 6 miles each. As always, we shared some laughs and shared some stories and had a good old time.

Eventually I made it to the finish line, which is the start of my third Marathon, turned around about midnight and headed back to the fire station where I was going to meet up with Kenny and his daughter Hannah. The plan was to rest there for at least a half an hour and get off my feet, eat something, regroup and then make our way to the starting line by 7:00 AM I met up with Ilya who had the most

305

important job, getting me to eat and drink and to the starting line on time and in one piece. I tried eating at the fire station and just couldn't swallow. I was nauseous and couldn't get anything down. I tried chia seeds thinking that when I put them in my smoothie it helps fill me up. They're packed with carbs, fiber and protein. This was a game changer. I was able to eat again a few minutes later. I knew I had to eat for fuel, but also to stay warm. I changed my sneakers for the 3rd time, and off we went.

The plan was to take our time to get to the actual starting line so I could save something in the tank for the official Marathon. Once we started again, we began moving a little bit faster and then we would back off. We made it to Hopkinton by 7:10 in the morning—10 minutes later than projected but no big deal. After saying goodbye and a big thank you to Ilya, I found my media contact for the BAA who was waiting for me. After doing three interviews one right after the other, finally I said I needed to get warm. I told him I needed a tent with fire or some sort of heat, otherwise I was going to become hypothermic. Shivering, I knew I needed to get some shelter soon, so I went to the Center school where the volunteers were staying in the basement prepping for the race. Having stayed there for over 2 hours to regroup, I got off my feet, drank coffee, ate bananas and consumed a few pounds of Swedish fish. My race started at 10:25 so at 10:20 I went out, hopped the barricade and got in the corral and started walking, then eventually started running.

My plan worked perfectly to this point and I couldn't believe that the time had come and I was actually running the marathon! The crowds were tremendous from the get-go. I ran the down hills hard

306

and once it leveled off I took it easy. My intention was to run the 2nd half of the race with a purpose. That's where I would see my family and friends. The rain was relentless and so were the 30-40 mile an hour head winds. It poured down many times; the harder it rained, the harder the crowd cheered as they fed off of it. The crowds got louder, which is pretty awesome to hear. It rained harder and they got louder. It energized me and I ran faster. You could just feel the energy. It was truly amazing. I shot by a few old friends, Jason Campbell in Framingham and Kevin Felton, too. Then once I got to Wellesley, I saw Kenny again, and then Jack and Kate Murphy. Each time I saw someone I knew it gave me a huge push. They were psyched to see me, but I was more psyched to see them.

I finally got to the Newton Firehouse for the last time after passing it three previous times and using it as an aid station. All I could do was stop and bow. They were super nice to let me use the fire station. I'm forever grateful. Some of them told me I'm a badass and I'm a hero. I quickly reminded them that they're the real heroes when that alarm goes off—they don't know what they're going to come out to. I'm just a silly runner. Then I started hitting the hills in Newton with a Vengeance. I couldn't wait to see my family and friends. And once I saw them it was just electric. I stopped for hugs, fist-pumps, high fives and quick conversations. The same deal—I fed off their energy and I would quickly take off and sprint up the hills. It is truly amazing what the human body is capable of. At this point, I still had plenty of energy left in my legs. At mile 20, I saw my family. I was shocked to see my parents, sisters, my niece and nephews, my wife and my son—my biggest fans! I was just ecstatic. I knew after seeing them I could ride that high all the way

307

to the finish line. I really ran the hills hard and for the most part ran the rest of the marathon hard.

Coming into Kenmore Square, seeing the Citgo sign I got emotional and then allllll cranked up. I slowed down passing Fenway Park to soak up the atmosphere and then started getting the crowds going. The louder they got the faster I ran. I literally sprinted to the finish line. I have completed the #bostonquad2018!!! I am really happy with the plan I put together. I will apply this towards #bostonquad2019 !

My parents waited for hours for me to pass by in the inclement weather. They hate the rain and the cold. Little did I know my dad would pass away five days later.

Four layers of pants and four layers on top.

Waltham, MA Running friends

My nephew Simon spectating.

The weather for Boston Quad 2019

The Johnny Kelly statue in Newton which I ran past four times.

Hereford St. Boston two-tenth of a mile left to finish
marathon nr. 4

Johnny Kelly Statue with Scot.

Alejandra, my sister Amy and friend Blanca, spectating.

Sebastian, Max and Jadyn

In the beginning of the 2018 Boston Quad

Interview with Steve Burton, Boston Channel 4 at the
starting line, after finishing three marathons that day.

Me, Sean Fraser and Sean Butler

Shenanigans

Hills of Newton

Snow...

Four marathons done – home and showered.

Glad to be done.

Newton Fire House

Newton Fire House

Run Based Boston

Finish Line which was my starting line.

Finish Line which was my starting line

Finish Line which was my starting line

ABC Arizona: Boston Marathon Quad April 2018

https://www.abc15.com/news/region-southeast-valley/tempe/tempe-man-to-run-boston-marathon-four-times-in-one-day

Pop Sugar fitness: Boston Marathon Quad April 2018

https://www.popsugar.com/fitness/Man-Runs-Boston-Marathon-4-Times-1-Day-44751463?utm_campaign=mobile_share&utm_medium=facebook&utm_source=popsugar

Boston.com article: Boston Marathon Quad April 2018

https://www.boston.com/sports/boston-marathon/2018/04/16/henry-ward-boston-marathon-quad?s_campaign=bcom%3Asocialflow%3Afacebook

CBS Boston: Boston Marathon Quad April 2018

http://boston.cbslocal.com/video/category/news/3846468-henry-ward-attempting-to-run-boston-marathon-course-4-times-in-24-hours/

Chapter 49
<u>Mesa Marathon Quad 2-8-19</u>

I really love the concept of the Boston Quad, so I decided to start a tradition out here in Arizona. I qualified for the Boston Marathon in January of 2018 which would mean I would be running the 2019 Boston Marathon. I said that if I qualified for Boston, I would do the Boston Marathon Quad again, and keep the tradition going. In February of 2019 I had the bright idea of doing the first ever Mesa Marathon Quad. Using the same concept, I would start at the expo and leave from there towards the starting line at Usery Mountain, turn around and run back to the finish line and turn around and run to the start line. With 45 minutes to spare I would run the official Mesa Marathon. I did the same thing in 2020 and will do the same thing in 2021.

"Have faith and find a way to just keep moving forward"
Like most ultras, there was a considerable amount of suffering during the Mesa Quads. All of a sudden, I am now known as a puker! In 2020 I threw up somewhere around 20 times. I experienced long spells of throwing up and dry heaving, which obviously depletes one of everything inside, including energy levels. I could not hold anything down; then the lowered energy levels would not allow me to move faster than a walk. I needed to stay on track in order to get to the starting line on time for the actual marathon, and that would be in jeopardy if I could not run at all! There were long stretches where I could not run and had doubts that I would make it in time, or be able to run again this day, period. It has been proven over and over again, that if we have faith, we can come back, we can run again! I rely on faith and I found a way to

327

make it to the start. I was able to quickly regroup there, eat something, and actually run most of the marathon. It is such a weird phenomenon, down and out then able to run again. What changed? A lot of people give up when it gets hard. This happens in life too. I believe they lose faith and let the evil voices in their head win. I like to think of it as having a good Fred Flintstone" on one shoulder, and a "bad Fred Flintstone" on the other shoulder. It is so much easier to listen to the voice that says, "This is hard, you are suffering, just quit", rather than listen to the voice that says, "Find a way to move forward, it is harder, but you can do it." There is a direct correlation to life and recovery from addiction. We need to have faith, trust the process, and find a way to put one foot in front of the other and just keep moving forward. Eventually we will get to where we need to be. It may be ugly, but if we have faith we can get there. I did the Boston Marathon Quad in 2019 and the weather was a little bit better. It absolutely down poured for hours over nigh. Of course it did!

24 Hour Desert Run Kiwanis Park 8-16-19
"Sleep deprived and nauseous was nothing compared to the hard times of addiction. I can get through this."
I chose to do a fundraiser for ADAA -The Anxiety Depression Association of America. I started at noon and finished at noon the following day. I literally did this on 2 hours of sleep. It was 115 degrees both days. It may be the hottest my internal temperature has ever been. This Friday probably 50 people came. Maybe half of them I met for the first time. Just like the other events that I've done it brought out some really amazing people. Some just wanted to see me offer words of encouragement, food or drinks or many shared

328

some gruesome miles. People opened up to me about their depression, about their anxiety about their addiction issues and we talked and talked and helped each other out. This fundraising concept raised $2,000 as well. Just like some of the other fundraising concepts I had done, this was a sufferfest! The heat was brutal! I threw up a lot and had little energy overnight, so I slept on a metal picnic table. I had serious doubts about running any more, but the sleep helped. I was able to close my eyes, mind, rest the body inside and out, and was able to eat again. Food is energy! There is no magic pill, but food gives you strength and my sleep deprived, overheated body was ready to go again! I was able to run and ran some quick miles pain free and no longer was nauseous. I cannot lie, I was ready to call it quits at midnight and my wife almost threw in the towel for me. I was hurting, but I was able to draw back into the hard times of addiction again, all the suffering I had back then and tell myself that this was nothing compared to those days and those nights. You got through that; you can get through this.

These are some of the fundraising concepts I did, and plan on doing many more.

"No matter how far down the scale we have gone, we will see how our experience can benefit others. That feeling of uselessness and self-pity will disappear. We will lose interest in selfish things and gain interest in our fellows. Self-seeking will slip away. Our whole attitude and outlook upon life will change. Fear of people and of economic insecurity will leave us. We will intuitively know how to handle situations which used to baffle

329

us. We will suddenly realize that God is doing for us what we could not do for ourselves."

Alcoholics Anonymous

Chapter 50

Running Without The Devil

"There is no cure for addiction, but it is treatable."

Today, I can honestly say that I am not free of my demons, but through hard work I am so much better off than I used to be. I often find myself having to restart my day, sometimes one hundred times. I am accountable for my actions; I am more grateful. I have a lot of work to do, and I believe that we are a work in progress. I strive to be the best me I can be. I remember one guy saying in an AA meeting why he keeps showing up, "Even though I am not drinking, I don't want to be an asshole." Addicts have a lot of baggage and character defects, and I am no different. I recognize them and try to work on them to better myself.

There is no cure for addiction, it is a disease like any other one. The good news is that it is treatable! Nobody is immune to it, no race, no age, no profession. The disease does not discriminate. Though I feel like I will never drink or use again, there is no guarantee. I am reminded every now and then that once an addict, always an addict. Last year, I went to the movies with Alejandra and Sebastian. I was going to go running after the movies and vowed not to buy or eat any popcorn because it trashes my stomach. Sebastian got a kids' combo which came with a small popcorn. The smell was killing me, so I begged him for just a few. I had three pieces, and before I knew it, I excused myself and found myself in the concession line without hesitation. This hit me like a ton of bricks! I walked away with a LARGE POPCORN! I was on autopilot. Nothing in moderation, not a small, I ordered a large. Take my money! This brought me back to the days of buying alcohol or drugs. I had shut down my defenses and let my guard down. I almost dumped out the popcorn like emptying a bottle. Just the smell and taste of three popcorn kernels had me hooked. I have an addictive personality that will never go away. I am glad I recognized it., For others, this could be a trigger or the steppingstone to going back out there drinking or using again.

"Everyone is capable of changing and everyone deserves a second chance."

I did not want to be the way I was. Addicts don't want to be the way they are. We are no different than people with other diseases. I hated myself for who I was, what I did, and that I did not have the strength to change or ask for help for years. There is a negative stigma that we are the stereotypical bums or homeless people, crooks, or just bad people. We are not. We are just broken and lost souls that need help and love. I believe everyone is capable of changing and everyone deserves a second chance. I also believe we can do anything that we want to, within reason. I will never be a professional football player, but if I wanted to be a doctor, if I put the time and wanted to do that, I could find a way and the money to accomplish that. If I could get sober, and I could quit smoking, I can do anything. Accomplishing those things have given me confidence as self-doubts creep in when I have a new challenge at work or school.

Chapter 51

How Running Has Helped Me

By now you know that running has helped me get through some really hard times. It helps me start my day off right, everything typically flows much better, and I am certainly more at ease and patient. This coming from someone who had zero patience! If I run after work, it helps to unwind and burn off the craziness of a hectic day.

Running helps me with staying in the moment, especially trail running. I am a scatterbrain and clumsy at times and you really need to stay focused on watching where you plant each foot. Nobody likes to stub their toes, or to fall. Everything in the desert has a sharp protective layer, so this is extra important for Arizona! It has helped me at work, as well. Here is a great example: we were very short handed at work and needed to chop 200 pounds of fruit and 200 pounds of potatoes nightly. Being a hyperactive busybody, I hate routine tasks and hate standing in the same place for periods of time. I have decent knife skills because of my years as a chef, so I decided to suck it up and do these tasks myself. I could not worry about how long it would take me to do these tasks or how my hand would feel after chopping fifty pounds or one hundred fifty pounds. I needed to just worry about how I felt at the moment and be as efficient as possible. It sucks, but if you dwell on it and keep saying so in your head you are never going to finish, and you will be hating life! This can put you in a bad mood and carry over to the next task, and the next one and ruin your day if you let it. Or, you have

333

the suck it up buttercup attitude and just find a way you push through and finish!

"What will you do with the extra time the pandemic has given you?"

The Covid-19 pandemic has been challenging to everyone and I am no different. I was furloughed twice, and we had just bought a house. Neither my wife nor myself was out of work. I knew that if we remain positive, embrace the forced change we would find a way to get through. Most days I start my day with a nice run or walk with Wini, my 11-pound Yorkshire Terrier, which sets me up for a great day! I promised to be flexible from the beginning of the pandemic. Back in April when this really started to unfold, I listened to a podcast about dealing with adversity, and specifically about dealing with the pandemic. It spoke about how to react and this really hit home. Someone had said, "There is no one way to deal with this pandemic." And the host agreed and countered that by stating that, "Correct, but there are certainly wrong ways to deal with it. One could abuse illicit drugs or alcohol, abuse their significant others, their children, mentally or physically, they could binge watch Netflix and eat chips all day on the couch, they could do all of these things and self-destruct. Or they could meditate, do yoga, fitness, run, walk, self-help, learn something new, read more, or simply do things they complained they did not have time to do before. Or they could spend more time with their loved ones they live with!" Imagine that? Be with the ones you love the most, more? I chose to take advantage of this time. I got to run more, write this book, it brought my family closer, I started a 5013c, just to name a few things. I always wished I had more time; now I have the time so I embraced it.

334

"We only get one chance in this life; be the best you can."
This pandemic is not going away soon, and let's face it, there could
be others. This is the time to "practice and learn from this one."
The ones that do not adapt and overcome, do not get help, that are
self-destructing could be descending on a downward spiral they
may not get out of. Life is hard, but we need to be our best to be
there for our families, and to make a difference in this world. If you
are struggling with anything, speak up and do not suffer in silence.
There are resources; there is help. Tell anyone, even a complete
stranger. Get out of your own head; sometimes it is not a great place
to go alone. You only get one chance in this life, be the best you, be
the best you can. We owe it to ourselves to see what we are capable
of.

Nobody saw the Covid-19 pandemic coming. God and sobriety
prepared me for this past year. As hard as this year was for
everyone, I already knew that if I have faith and keep listening to
God, good things will come of this. God taught me in sobriety to
continue working on myself, continue to strengthen my
relationships, and to be the best me and be of service to others. I
just continued doing this, lived in the moment, and was not as
stressed as most others. I tried to live in the moment, go with the
flow, and since I understand most of the pandemic is not in my
control, I chose to only control what I can. I basically worked for 4
months on and off this past year, and eventually was let go from my
job. I was 100% okay with that; God has bigger plans for me that I

335

know from having faith, and that I know from my relationship with God. Without him in my life, I would be nothing.

I run and do some of the "crazy things" I do because I can. I was given a gift, and if God gives you a gift, do not waste those gifts. I applaud people that find their calling or their niche or are simply happy doing what they do. If they love or excel at knitting, chess, tiddlywinks, soccer, or crosswords puzzles, more power to them. If it makes them happy doing those things and they share their experiences, tips, and passion I applaud them. I am 50, I still love WWE wrestling, the Simpsons, Impractical Jokers. Is there something wrong with that if it makes me happy? I think not, you be you.

I am very fortunate to have a team of companies that have helped me be me! I was in love with **Inknburn** www.inknburn.com the first time I saw their products. I ran into the 2014 Boston Marathon expo, and was able to buy my first Inknburn singlet, the "Stars and Stripes." Their unique designs are perfect for my outgoing personality and compliment my flare! I was lucky enough to become an ambassador, and then invited to be on the Elite Team. Never in my wildest dreams did I envision this happening. I believe in work, being outgoing, and sharing a brand that you 100% believe in. Thank you, Megan and Inknburn for everything you have done for me! I cannot say enough great things about your company, about you, and about your best in business athletic wear! Thank you **Trail Toes** www.trailtoes.com for taking care of my blistered feet, and really making some killer products that I use all the time.

336

Besides the cream, they make tire pulling kits, foot care kits, dog leashes, gear bags and other handmade items. Thank you, Vincent. You rock!

Tailwind Nutrition (www.tailwindnutrition.com) always had my back! Thank you, Maggie and Tailwind for all your generosity and supplying me with all my electrolytes and nutrition!

Chapter 52

No Finish Line

What's Next for YOU?

Being an addict and an alcoholic, sometimes I feel like there is no finish line. It is not like I am not happy, grateful or proud of my successes or accomplishments, or psyched to knock off a bucket list item race, but after the event is over, I am left with the "what's next feeling, or how can I top that one?" I believe in growth, and with growth there needs to be a progression. Just like when I did the Boston Marathon double, the next step was the quad.

I aspire to run Badwater 135. "The World's Toughest Foot Race"

Covering 135 miles (217km) non-stop from Death Valley to Mt. Whitney, CA, the Badwater® 135 is the most demanding and extreme running race offered anywhere on the planet. The start line is at Badwater Basin, Death Valley, which marks the lowest elevation in North America at 280' (85m) below sea level. The race finishes at Whitney Portal at 8,300' (2530m), which is the trailhead to the Mt. Whitney summit, the highest point in the contiguous United States. The Badwater 135 course covers three mountain ranges for a total of 14,600' (4450m) of cumulative vertical ascent and 6,100' (1859m) of cumulative descent. Competitors travel through places or landmarks with names like Mushroom Rock, Furnace Creek, Salt Creek, Devil's Cornfield, Devil's Golf Course, Stovepipe Wells, Panamint Springs, Darwin, Keeler, Lone Pine, Alabama Hills, and the Sierra Nevada. The average temperature is 120 degrees ,and the race is always in July. I have the minimum qualifications and will continue to apply to gain entry!

338

In May 2021 will be running Aravaipa's inaugural Cocodona 250. Cocodona is the brainchild of Jamil Coury, brought to life by Aravaipa Running – linking together some of the most iconic trails and towns in Arizona for one monumental undertaking of 250 consecutive miles. Join us May 3-8, 2021 for the inaugural running of this life altering ultramarathon. The Cocodona Trail is a curated route through central Arizona linking historic towns and paths off the beaten path. The rich history of the towns linked up through little traveled ranges makes this a one-of-a-kind tour of Arizona. From the beauty of the Sonoran Desert, through canyons and pine forests this is a magical route. The accomplishment of traveling the Cocodona Trail on foot will be one of the most life changing and epic journeys of an endurance athlete's career. We envision this as a once in a lifetime experience and the pinnacle endurance challenge in North America.

Cocodona 250 takes runners from Black Canyon City up into the Bradshaw Mountains – an area steeped in gold mining lore – to the historic town of Crown King. The course then traverses more of the Bradshaws, up and over Mount Union, and snakes down into Prescott where it cuts straight through town on Whiskey Row and out into the iconic Granite Dells. From Prescott the course heads up and over Mingus Mountain into the town of Jerome and onward through Sedona, experiencing a mix of stunning red rock formations and high desert vistas. As runners leave Sedona, the course starts to get into the pines of Flagstaff, finishing up and over Mt Elden and into downtown Flagstaff. It is an extraordinary undertaking and gives runners an incredible point-to-point experience through some of the best landscapes that Arizona has to offer.

Like I said, there is no finish line, but I may retire after this one! This will be the biggest fitness challenge for next year! I have been through far worse; I can get through this.

What's Next?

One of the things that I am doing to give back as part of my recovery is to teach and coach others. I have started my own running and fitness coaching business called Henry Ward Endurance Coaching. I am focusing on helping people push through their perceived barriers and crushing their goals in the process. I am teaching people that their bodies will follow their minds and their minds are limitless. Through cross training and training the mind's people can accomplish the unimaginable. It starts with what I call "Couch to 5K"; getting people moving from a sedentary lifestyle—from walking to running; then to doing a Half marathon and a marathon if they wish. It will be done mostly virtually, online, with all sessions individually. As a chef, I can also do local package meals and prep. For those seeking to have a healthy diet, home cooked. You can go all-inclusive or a la carte. A new dedicated website will soon follow.

And now for the BIG NEWS! I started my own charity in Sept of 2020 during the pandemic. It's a non-profit called appropriately Running Without the Devil. I am raising money for those who cannot afford treatment and aftercare. Visit: www.runningwithoutthedevil.com

341

Mission: To help people who are suffering from addiction get the treatment and aftercare they need, and to emphasize running and fitness as a critical part of their recovery and maintenance plans.

Vision: To help remove the negative stigma associated with addiction.Alcoholics and addicts do not want to be the way they are. It is a disease without a cure, but with treatment and aftercare we can recover and often thrive in society.

Goals: To build a community and network of advocates for recovery from addiction. We will work together to raise funds and awareness to help as many alcoholics and addicts as possible.

TO THE ADDICT HATERS

I know that addiction is hard for you to understand. It was hard for me to understand too and I suffer from it. I know you think addiction isn't a disease, it's a CHOICE. What if I told you that YOU MADE THE SAME CHOICE! Confused? When you were a teen did you ever smoke pot, have a drink, drop acid or snort a line? Even just once, because if you did, YOU MADE THE SAME CHOICE. The only difference is you were lucky. You were able to stop - a person with the disease isn't.

People with the disease of addiction have a disorder. ENDORPHINS are a chemical produced by the brain. It is what makes us feel pleasure. It also provides an overall feeling of well being. The average person has a level of **80** which ensures that they are motivated, happy and basically content. Those that suffer from addiction have an average of **40** So when they use, their levels for the FIRST TIME are normal or above. Their brain naturally seeks more. Addiction effects the part of the brain that tells you that you are hungry, go eat. Your primal needs. If you have the disease of addiction your brain sends itself messages just to use - URGENT MESSAGES. Like it would to get you to eat if you were starving!

343

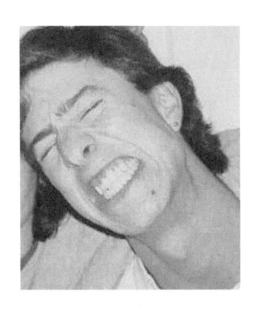

About the Author

Henry Ward grew up in Waltham, Massachusetts and currently resides in Chandler, Arizona with his wife Alejandra and his son Sebastian. After graduating from culinary school, his professional background has included years of work in the food service industry, as a chef and in various supervisory and managerial roles. He was chosen to work at the Beijing Olympics by his former employer.

Through treatment, aftercare, personal self-development and running, he is successfully battling his demons of addiction. Henry has demonstrated the power of recovery, having run numerous marathons and ultra-marathons as fundraisers both in the U.S. and overseas. He has started Running Without the Devil, a 501C3 charity to raise money for those unable to afford treatment for addiction.
www.RunningWithouttheDevil.com

Made in the USA
Middletown, DE
16 January 2025

69658264R00195